EXPLORING THE NORFOLK MARKET TOWN

Further details of Poppyland Publishing titles can be found at
www.poppyland.co.uk
where clicking on the 'Support and Resources' button
will lead to pages specially compiled to support this title.

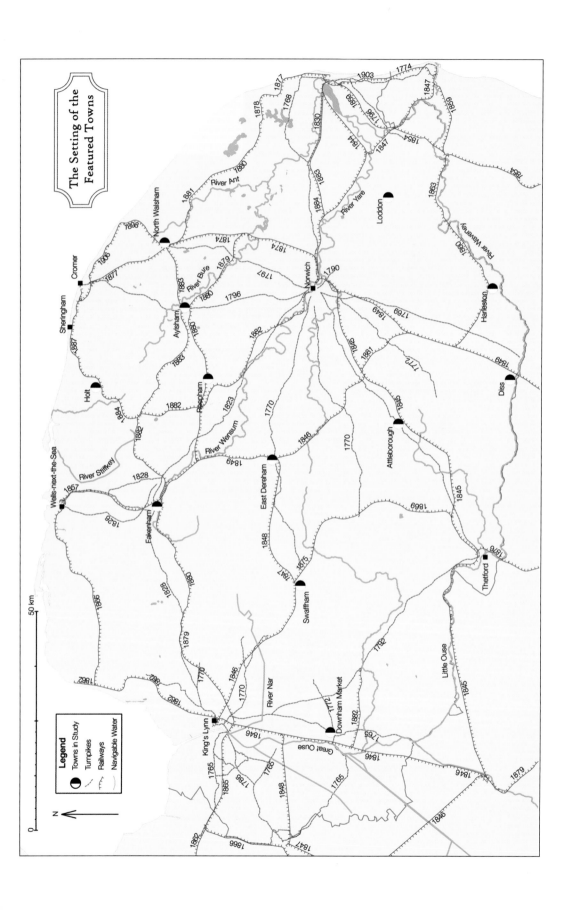

The Setting of the Featured Towns

Legend
- Towns in Study
- Turnpikes
- Railways
- Navigable Water

Exploring the Norfolk Market Town

Christopher Barringer

POPPYLAND PUBLISHING

EXPLORING
THE NORFOLK
MARKET TOWN

Copyright © 2011 Christopher Barringer

First published 2011

ISBN 0 946148 93 6

Published by Poppyland Publishing, Cromer, NR27 9AN

Picture credits

Fakenham Local History Society: pages 65, 70
James Mindham redrew the plans on pages 17, 20, 29, 57, 85
Ruth Murray redrew the maps and plans on pages 12, 13, 15, 21, 24, 25 (bottom), 26, 32, 36, 41, 42, 45, 48, 55, 58 (top), 61, 62, 66, 75, 83, 86, 92, 95, 96, 101, 102, 105, 111, 118, 127
Norfolk Record Office: 113 (top)
Mike Page: pages 6 (bottom), 11, 53, 91, 113, 121
Christopher Pipe/Watermark: pages 22, 28, 49 (priory, Bridge Street), 69, 87 (bottom), 89, 104 (top), 109 (top)
Poppyland collection: 104 (middle)
Poppyland Photos: pages 6 (top), 23, 100, 104 (bottom), 105 (top), 109 (bottom), 114, 115 (top left), 116 (top), 117 (top & middle), 125, 130 (bottom), 132
Poppyland Publishing: pages 8, 25 (top), 50, 54, 58 (bottom), 67, 68, 73, 77, 93, 106, 112
Other photographs are by the author

Designed and typeset in 10 on 12pt Legacy Sans by Watermark, Cromer

Printed in the EU by Latitude Press Ltd

Other titles in the Norfolk Origins series:
1: Hunters to First Farmers (published 1981)
2: Roads and Tracks (published 1983; 2nd edition 2008)
3: Celtic Fire and Roman Rule (1987; 3rd edition 2003)
4: The North Folk: Angles, Saxons & Danes (published 1990)
5: Deserted Villages in Norfolk (published 1996)
6: Changing Agriculture in Georgian & Victorian Norfolk (published 2002)
7: The Norfolk Dialect (published 2003)
8: Exploring the Norfolk Village (published 2005)

Preface

This study of market towns is a follow-up to my examination of the story of 15 villages in *Exploring the Norfolk Village*. It is also a sample of some of the market towns that have particularly interested me. Thetford, Great Yarmouth, King's Lynn and Wymondham have all had recently published studies giving considerable detail of their histories. Those I have chosen have in part selected themselves because it was my good fortune to have been invited by University Extra-Mural or WEA groups to explore with them various aspects of their histories. References to any such studies are made in the relevant chapters. In 43 years teaching in Norfolk it has been a delight to meet with such student groups out of which have come many long term friendships.

Another privilege has been to have worked with many interesting and stimulating colleagues whilst teaching these groups for the University of Cambridge and later that of East Anglia. Two colleagues with whom I have enjoyed many long hours in discussion and in the field have been Dr David Dymond, my counterpart in Suffolk, and David Yaxley who was for many years tutor organiser for the WEA in Norfolk. As a member of the Scole Committee and as a President of the Council of the Norfolk and Norwich Archaeological Society I have had the added privilege of meeting so many of those engaged in research into the archaeology, landscape history and history of the county. The volumes of *East Anglian Archaeology*, the *Norfolk Record Society* and *Norfolk Archaeology* have been major quarries for much information.

My thanks go also to the staffs of the Norfolk Record Office, the Norfolk Heritage Centre and the Centre of East Anglian Studies for their friendly interest in and help with my researches.

I am grateful to Peter Stibbons for asking me to follow up the 'villages' and to Christopher Pipe for his editing assistance, Ruth Murray for 30 of the maps and James Mindham for five further maps. Finally, my wife Charlotte has ably processed the whole text, making many helpful comments as she did so.

I would like to dedicate this book to the memories of my father Maurice and my mother Essie Barringer. They started me off on all this.

RIGHT: *Downham Market, set beside the Great Ouse river, its straighter relief channel (cut in the 1950s) and the 1847 railway line from Ely to Kings Lynn.*

BELOW: *Diss, uniquely centred on its very deep mere.*

Contents

The landscapes influencing Norfolk's market towns: **1.** *A new drain cut into deep peat at Wormegay.* **2.** *Grazing in a meadow at Whitwell – rich grazing was also vital to the cattle-rearing wealth of Diss and Harleston in the Waveney valley.* **3.** *Hickling Broad, created by the digging of peat for Norwich Cathedral and for St Benet's Abbey (whose market town was North Walsham).* **4.** *Drained fen washland in the Bedford Levels.* **5.** *East Wretham: a birch and heather scene typical of the Breckland south and west of Swaffham, and of the area around Holt.* **6.** *Ashwellthorpe Wood, surviving ancient woodland; the towns of the wet boulder clay plateau used timber for their early buildings.*

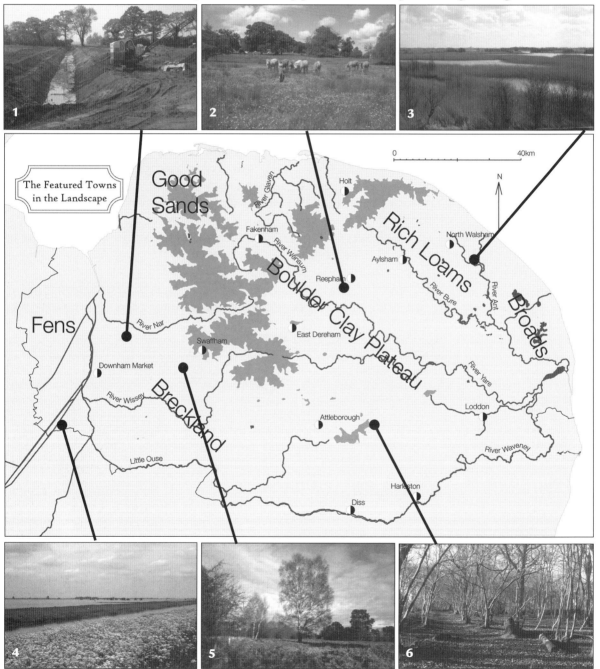

Introduction

Norfolk is a county of over 600 villages and some two dozen market towns. Each of these towns and the villages that focus on it has a long history. Norfolk is an old county in terms of the length of time man has been using it and this still shows from its flint workings at Grimes Graves to its Norman churches, its Georgian rectories and its great landscaped estates of the 18th century. Its landscape carries the marks of many people and many events. This book looks at a dozen of its smaller market towns in an attempt to show what makes them distinctive.

The physical variety of Norfolk, discussed in *Exploring the Norfolk Village,* also shows in the towns. There is a striking division between the corn and sheep country in which Swaffham lies and the wood pasture country in which Diss and Harleston are situated with their surviving timber buildings and their links to the rearing of cattle on the river marshes. This variety is especially noticeable at Downham Market where the sheep and barley uplands meet what was once the marsh land of the Fens. Holt and Fakenham, close to the sea at Cley and Wells, had easy access to Europe. Aylsham and North Walsham were both centres of the cloth trade and perhaps more closely linked to Norwich than the other towns.

Particular families or individuals have at some time also exercised local influence. The Hobarts, early at Loddon and later at Aylsham, played a major role in the appearance of the two towns. The Pastons, long influential in north east Norfolk, left their mark on North Walsham in both school and church. Even earlier in their histories the Abbeys of St Benet, Bromholm and Ely exercised their authority over North Walsham and East Dereham as well as over many of their neighbouring villages.

Communities too altered their own environments. The people of Swaffham and Redenhall (Harleston) who united to rebuild their churches demonstrated a feeling of local pride and faith. This trend continued later as they provided civic meeting places, almshouses and schools for their inhabitants until central government legislation began to impose more uniformity.

Market towns did have many things in common; besides the markets, there were local trades and crafts, and tanning, malting and brewing were important local industries. The arrival of the turnpikes, railways and one or two small navigations affected and still affect the towns through which they ran. Diss and Downham Market both have electrified railways but the others have seen them come and go providing local and distinctive influences.

The view of Diss on its hill above the Mere, of the shattered tower of North Walsham church, of Swaffham's Georgian façades, of the Waveney meadows by Harleston and the sweep of the Bure Valley around Aylsham which stands high above it, remain with us if we spend any time exploring these towns.

Note on units of measurement

LAND

The acre, equivalent to 0.4 of the modern hectare, is divided into four roods, each of 40 perches

MONEY

The pound (£) consists of twenty shillings (s) each of 12 pence (d).

Attleborough chronology

7th–8th century	Bunn's Bank
AD 1000	Saxon church
1086	Attleborough, three manors – Attleborough, the Other Attleborough and Alfred's
1146	Old Buckenham Priory founded by William d'Albini
1150	The Norman church of Attleborough
1226	Market charter
1297	South chapel to the church – Sir William Mortimer
1310	Charter for fair – Constantine Mortimer
1378	Chaunticlere's chapel on the north side of the tower
1387	College of the Holy Cross founded by Sir Robert de Mortimer
1420	Sir John Ratcliffe, Knight of the Garter
1436	The church nave and aisles built to west of tower
	Church choir reserved for the College
1461	Sir John Ratcliffe killed at Ferrybridge in the Wars of the Roses
1475	Rood screen separated College from parish church
1541	Destruction of the chancel and the College
1569	Town Lands charity established
1559	Town fire
1613–38	John Forbie, Rector of both parts of the Rectory Manor
1651	Ratcliffe sold the manor to Bickley
1664	366 hearths, population approximately 1647
1675	Sir Edwin Rich gave £200 for the repair of the Wymondham to Attleborough road
1678	Narford's Charity established to found a school
1695	Wymondham to Attleborough turnpike
1766	Norwich to Thetford turnpike
1801	Population 1,333
1812	Enclosure Act, the Award in 1815
1825	Baptist chapel built
1834	Wayland Union workhouse built at Rockland
1838	Tithe map and tithe commutation
1840	Elementary school
1845	Norwich to Thetford railway
1851	Population 2,324
1872	Wesleyan chapel on Station Road; Gaymer's cider factory opens; new Wayland workhouse
1901	Methodist church built
1971	Population 4,079
1974	Local government reorganisation – Breckland District Council
2001	Population 9,702

Attleborough

Attleborough lay in the hundred of Shropham which stretched for 14 miles to the edge of Thetford; its southern boundary was defined by the Little Ouse and the Thet. It abutted Wayland and Forehoe hundreds to the north and east. It is not clear why the hundred should have been named after Shropham rather than Attle-borough because Attleborough always seems to have been the most important place in the hundred from the time of the Conquest. The *Historical Atlas of Norfolk,* however, shows that Quidenham had importance in the mid-Saxon period with many finds of coins and metalwork. Attleborough lies on the main road from Norwich to Thetford which then leads on to London via Bury. A small stream drains the shallow valley from the Hall via the hamlet of Baconsthorpe to flow west and unite with other small streams to form the river Thet. It lies on the border zone between the boulder clay plateau and the sands of Breckland.

Attleborough in the early twenty-first century, looking west.

One theme of this account is the impact of this important west–east route on

the growth and character of the town. However, a second theme is the ownership of the main manor of Attleborough Mortimers and its significance for the development of the church and its associated college. The families of Mortimer and their successors, the Ratcliffes, both had wider national significance than might be expected.

Three major sources exist for the study of Attleborough: R. H. Mason's *History of Norfolk* (1885), the first volume of Francis Blomefield's *Essay towards a Topographical History of the County of Norfolk (1805)* and J. T. Barrett's *Memorials of the Parochial Church . . . of Attleborough (1848)* and these have provided much helpful material for the first part of this account. Blomefield provided an unusually detailed, if hypothetical, discussion of Attleborough's origins. 'This place, without doubt,' he says, 'hath been very famous in early times, as all authors that speak of it unanimously agree.' He quotes John Brome, a Thetford monk, whose history survived at Corpus Christi College, Cambridge, as saying 'it was some time not only a city but the metropolis of all Norfolk, founded by Atlinga, then king of that province'.

The difficulty is that Domesday Book gives no clue as to any previous borough having existed. However, it does recognise Attleborough and 'the other Attleburgh' in two surprisingly similar descriptions, both being held by Roger, son of Rainard, in 1086. The two demesnes (manor estates) were very similar. Was a larger holding split equally or was this a confusion in the recording? Attleborough had 21 freemen, the Other had 17; otherwise both had the same value and they came under one spatial description of two leagues in length and one league in width (i.e. three miles by one and a half miles), the size of the existing parish. Alfred's, the third holding, was very much smaller.

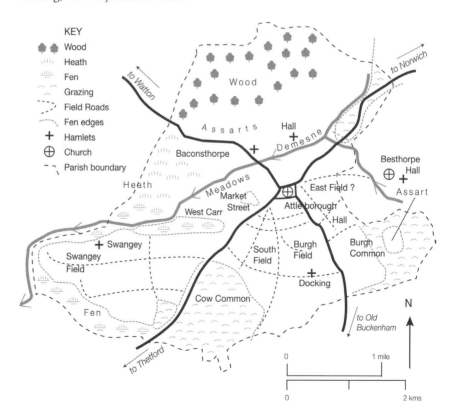

Some medieval components of Attleborough.

The parish is a big one. The elements of a park and of Attleborough wood were both clearly related to Attleborough Hall. Archaeological evidence, as revealed by the *Historical Atlas of Norfolk,* is not strong in this area. A probable Roman road ran from west to east close to the north of the town. This road ran from Brettenham towards either Crownthorpe or Caistor St Edmund. Archaeologically this is a feature that merits further investigation. A second feature is that of Bunn's Bank, an earthwork that edges the south and south-eastern sides of the parish. This bank and ditch have never been satisfactorily explained, it has been suggested that it might be the limit of a former territorial unit; if so, for what period? More recently perhaps it might have been the northern boundary of the Buckenham Priory deer park.

This brings us to the very complex manorial structure of Attleborough. Blomefield listed the manors as follows:

> Plasset or Plassinghall
> Baconsthorpe, Crows Hall or Copsey Manor
> Chaunticlers or Chancellors with two thirds of the advowson
> Attleborough Mortimers with one third of the advowson
> The Great Rectory Manor
> Little Rectory Manor

Attleborough Mortimers was the most important of these and Blomefield devoted a long account to the Mortimer family,[1] the relevant members of which are mentioned below.

Attleborough church

The history of Attleborough church is an introduction to the history of the town as well. The church dominates the east end of the town lying to the south of the main road. It is a striking building with its eastern tower and fine Decorated style aisle windows and great west window. An east tower is of course very odd. As the plan shows, it was originally a central tower: the chancel was demolished when the College occupying it was dissolved by Henry VIII.

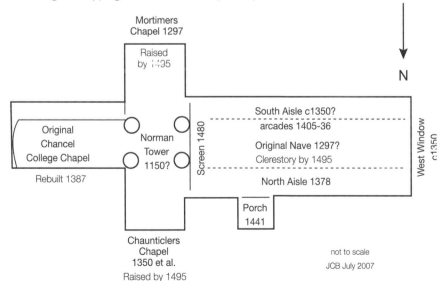

The evolution of Attleborough church.

The massive piers of the tower and two small Norman windows looking down into the present nave are remnants of a former major building.

The original church may have been Saxon but no architectural evidence of this survives and no church was mentioned in Domesday Book. What does survive is the fine base and first storey of a tower which is of high quality Norman work, c. 1150. The Mortimer chapel and Chaunticlere's chapel provide the explanations for the south and north transepts respectively, and the rebuilding of the nave and aisles are replacements for what presumably was a Norman nave, reflecting the Ratcliffe phase of ownership, as does that of the porch.

The Mortimer family by 1089 had links with Attleborough. They held Attleborough and many other manors from Earl Warenne as a holding of six knights' fees. By 1263 Sir William Mortimer held a manor house, 243 acres of land, 469 acres of wood, a windmill and £43 in rents in Attleborough. The manor house was presumably on the site of the present day Attleborough Hall. The family line was continued by successive Constantine de Mortimers, of whom the second was MP for Norfolk eight times between 1321 and 1338; his brother, Sir Robert de Mortimer, was also an MP for Norfolk from 1363 to 1366 and in 1372. This Sir Robert founded the Chantry of the Holy Cross (the College) and was buried in the chancel in 1387. Sir Robert married a Margaret Fastolf and his son, Sir Thomas, married Mary Park who in turn married John Fastolf and was mother of the famous Sir John. This Sir Thomas had three daughters of whom Cecily married Sir John de Herling and then in 1411 married John Ratcliffe of Attleborough to whom she left her estate. The daughters and their respective spouses were burdened with completing the work on the College.

John Ratcliffe Esq had a distinguished son, Sir John Ratcliffe, who was made a Knight of the Garter in 1425 and was buried in Attleborough church in 1438. He served in a number of military campaigns and died being owed £7,013 for his services to Henry VI in France. Sir John's son, a second John, was killed at Ferrybridge in 1461 at one of the battles of the Wars of the Roses, having by marriage become Lord Fitzwalter. This title was lost by the next John but regained by his son Sir Robert KG as the Viscount Fitzwalter, Earl of Sussex, who in 1541 was awarded the College and its lands at the Dissolution. His tomb in Boreham church in Essex is shared with two other Earls of Essex: it is of alabaster, dated 1589; it cost £266 13s 4d.[2] The Ratcliffes, as Earls of Sussex, continued to hold Attleborough until they sold it c. 1650 to Sir Francis Bickley.

The impact of these two families on the town of Attleborough and in particular on the church was important. When Sir Robert founded the College in 1387 the old chancel of the church to the east of the tower was rebuilt with aisles and the great screen set up to separate the College from the parish church in the nave. The aisles were built in the Decorated style as was the west window. In 1441 Sir John Ratcliffe built a two-storey porch on the north side of the church facing the town.

The College was founded with four priests to celebrate the memory of the Mortimer family and also of the later Ratcliffes. There was a separate building for the domestic quarters of the priests; there is some doubt as to its exact location. A building which was formerly on the site of the present car park was known as College House and it may be that this was a survival of at least part of the College building.[3] Barrett noted that the remains of the chantry were 41 feet 9 inches (12.7 m) from east to west and 45 feet 9 inches (13.9 m) from north to south. Walls were standing until *c.* 1800 when he commented that they were robbed for fabric to repair the highway![4]

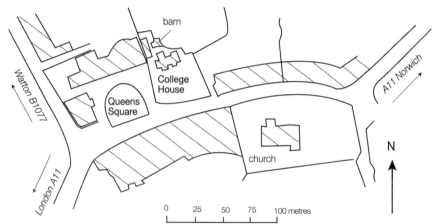

Although much of College House was built in brick, or had a brick skin, parts of its structure visible during demolition in 1972 were clearly much older.

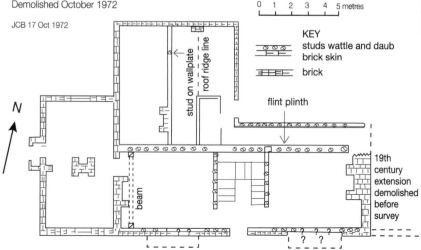

College House Attleborough
Demolished October 1972

JCB 17 Oct 1972

KEY
studs wattle and daub
brick skin
brick

flint plinth

19th century extension demolished before survey

Charities and the poor

The 17th and 18th centuries saw, as in most of the other towns discussed, new concerns for education and for helping the poor. In 1678 Rev Henry Nerford gave a messuage and eight acres in Baconsthorpe to provide an income to pay a school-master to teach grammar. He had to be a graduate of one of the universities and a 'person well learned and sober and of unblameable conversation' and he was to teach six poor children at no cost to them and they were to be known as Mr Nerford's scholars. At the enclosure of 1815 a further half acre of land was added to the bequest. In 1830 it was noted that the income was not enough to attract a graduate.[5]

Henry Nerford also gave a messuage and four acres for an income to provide free bread for six poor widows. In 1569, 22 pieces of land in Attleborough totalling 29 acres were given to the town to offset the costs of its maintenance. Various church lands added to by the enclosure award were allocated for a variety of charitable purposes. Sir Francis Bickley left a close in 1760 from which income was to be used for distribution to the poor on Christmas Day.

The poor rate of Attleborough was, of course, gathered from the late 16th century but the various bequests listed above all helped to fill small gaps in the lives of the poor. In 1835 Attleborough and the new union of Wayland had to put the national New Poor Law legislation into operation. The Poor Law commissioner, Sir Edward Parry, attended the first meeting of the guardians of the newly created union which consisted of 12 Shropham parishes and all but three of those in Wayland Hundred. Medieval units were being broken up and assembled into new patterns. The major problem the guardians faced was that of deciding where to site a union workhouse to replace the various parish workhouses that had existed from 1600.

The minutes of the first meeting, held at the Angel Inn in Larling on 21st September, record that:

> Sir Edward Parry having suggested it was desirable for the Board to come to a resolution as soon as possible that a workhouse sufficient for the purpose of the union should be erected, several guardians expressed themselves to be unprepared to enter into the question, not being yet in possession of any information of the subject.[6]

However, by 12th November a report of the Workhouse Committee noted that nine offers of land for a site had been made. Mr Robert Leeder offered a piece of land in Rockland St Andrew near the street containing two acres, one rood and 34 perches (about one hectare) at £120. This offer was accepted and it was agreed to advertise for plans for a workhouse for 200 people.

On 28th January 1836 nine plans were submitted and it was agreed to accept the plans of the well known London architect W. J. Donthorne. Mr John Mann suggested that the walls after the first 3 feet (0.9 m) should be made of clay, that timber should be of the best red wood deal and the roof of slate. After discussion it was agreed that the walls be of solid clay rather than of clay lump!

On 8th February 1836 discussions were taking place as to the employment of the poor; various trustees offered land on which they could work. As a result of Sir Edward's visit the guardians were spurred into activity and this workhouse lasted until the new Wayland workhouse (now Wayland hospital) was built.

By the 1830s the prosperity of farming, which had been bolstered by the French wars, was declining. Bread riots were taking place by 1816 as corn prices rose, followed by a rise in the cost of bread. The first machines were being introduced by 1830 and labourers felt that they threatened their work. Rev. F. Franklin of Attleborough was rector and, perhaps because he was lord of the rectory manors, was regarded with some suspicion by the labourers. The *Norfolk Chronicle* of 11th December 1830 reported that

> *The family of the Rev F. Franklin were disturbed by an assemblage of riotous persons about 10 o'clock on Saturday evening; they continued their yells and execration till about 3 o'clock on Sunday morning when they insisted on Mr Franklin's coming down and showing them where a hand chaff engine was kept which they threatened immediately to destroy.*

On the following day a parish meeting discussed the possibility of increasing labourers' wages and this was agreed as was a reduction of tithes. This proved insufficient and the situation became more serious. An assembled mob destroyed the chaff engine and two others nearby. The magistrate went to Wymondham for military help and an officer with 12 men arrived and read the Riot Act. The threat of opening fire on the rioters was sufficient to quieten them.

The town

After the loss of the College the market place was, as it had always been, the focal point for traffic along the main Thetford to Norwich road.

Along Exchange Street would have been a fringe of timber-framed cottages, probably thatched, until the 18th century. Town houses surrounding the small market place do not reach the standard of those of Swaffham or Aylsham. A

Attleborough
Tithe Map 1838
(extract)

N

Houses
Other Buildings

The tithe map shows a small market place just to the west of the church and a number of routes splayed off to Besthorpe, Buckenham, East Harling and Watton as well as the main Norwich to Thetford road. The plan was more linear than those of Aylsham or North Walsham but similar to Harleston. (Redrawn from tithe map 84 in the Norfolk Record Office.)

RIGHT: *Attleborough's former Corn Hall.*

The thatched cottage in Connaught Road is the best survivor of the old cottages but several of the public houses in Exchange Street such as the Griffin survive with timber frame structures.

Corn Hall was established in 1863 and Nonconformist chapels were built for the Baptists (1833), Quakers and Methodists. The great road, the modern A11, provided the thread along which Attleborough grew. The weight of traffic of carts and of movement of stock severely damaged it. The post-medieval system of maintaining roads was built around the Justices of the Peace who had the authority to compel parish surveyors of highways to pay for their repair. Major routes imposed a heavy drain on the resources of small parishes in the 17th and 18th centuries.

Ogilby's route map of 1675 showed that Attleborough and Thetford lay on the road from London to Norwich.[7] In 1695 a turnpike was established between

Wymondham and Attleborough so that the income from travellers paid the cost of maintaining the road as well as benefiting the investors. Parishes still had to contribute labour and materials at the request of the trustees of the turnpike. A sequence of acts then extended the authority of the trustees and added to the length of the turnpike until, by 1767, it stretched from the Town Close in Norwich to the chalk pits in Thetford. An act of 1741 noted that the road had benefited from tolls:

> Great progress hath been made in repairing the said road . . . yet by reason of extraordinary decay of the said road and the nature of the soil thereof (which is chiefly clay) and the difficulty of getting proper materials for the said road.

The road still needed repairs!

A new term of authority was asked for by the trustees in order to maintain the road.[8] These measures did not solve all the problems and as late as 1860 Thomas Beevor JP, a trustee, received a letter complaining of the 'dilapidated state of the turnpike through the town of Attleborough, the said road not having been properly repaired for several years past'.[9] The cost of maintaining major roads became too heavy for turnpike trusts and by 1888 all of them had been dissolved and the new County Council took over their maintenance. This process has continued and the A11 is now the responsibility of the Highways Agency. The latest result of the sheer pressure of traffic has been the building of a northern bypass to the whole length of the built-up area, but this has still not solved the problem of north–south traffic through the town. The 'great road' is the life blood of the town but a cause of congestion still.

A sale notice in 1831 for The Cock, 'an old established inn and posting house', noted that it was the only posting house in Attleborough. It had 11 sleeping rooms and stabling in the yard for 50 horses.[10] White's Directory of 1845 carried a note that:

> Coaches, vans etc. to Norwich, London, Thetford, Cambridge etc. called daily at the Attleborough inns but they no doubt will be discontinued when the railway is opened in the summer of 1845.

Large numbers of coach and cart horses became redundant and the coaching inns in Attleborough saw a reduction in trade but the railway provided a location for new businesses. One example of this was the development of the cider making firm of Gaymers.[11] In 1898 their private ledger listed cider sales of £11,100 and those for apples at £223, and by 1910 their cider sales were £40,000. Kelly's 1908 Directory noted that the London address of the firm was Arch 23, Bishopsgate Goods Station GER, a clear reflection of the importance of the railway to the firm. Gaymers finally closed their Attleborough premises c. 1980, the land values by then making the site attractive for more industry or housing. Also at the station by 1908 were Long Mann & Co, maltsters, corncrushers, beer, corn, coal, malt, hops, seeds, linseed and rape cake dealers. Coller & Sons were also corn, coal, cake and seed merchants and the Anglo-American oil company were also at the station. These activities all reflect the rural, agricultural nature of the area.

Attleborough in 2010 is facing a major planning issue. Having had an allocation for more housing the issue arises as whether to grow east and west within

Attleborough market place, showing a mixture of building periods.

Attleborough
Enclosure Map 1815
(extract)

0   5   10
Chains

N

Wm Cockell Esq

W.C. Cadywold

J. Lincoln

Ann Sheldrake

Rev Fairfax Franklin

Jonathan Cooper

Rev Fairfax Franklin

Glebe

Back Street

Hy Johnson

Crowshall

Clay Pit

Wm Ripper Coe

Houses

Other Buildings

Water

the A11/railway lozenge or to grow south of the railway. Attleborough's situation, astride a main route in which the railway is becoming more important, is still influencing its future growth.

The enclosure of the commons

As the map shows Attleborough parish had a fringe of commons. The line of the great road had long stretches of common to the south-west and north-east and Market Street Common up against the town. These all reflect the flow of people and stock, the latter needing grazing space. Swangey Field, a spur of upland, had wet commons lapping it and the former Attleborough Wood had several small greens carved out of it. Ling Common was on sandy soils and Borough Common served the tenants of the common field called Borough Field. This large acreage of commons was further complicated by areas over which rights of half-year grazing, or shack (grazing after harvest), extended. As the Act stated,

> *Whereas the said commons and waste grounds, in their present state and condition, yield very little profit to the several persons interested therein; and the said Open Fields, Half-year Lands, Shack Lands and Fen, are inconveniently situated for their respective owners and proprietors thereof, and it would be greatly advantageous to the several persons interested in the premises, if the rights of sheep walk and common in, over and upon the said half-year lands, shack lands, fens, commons and waste grounds were extinguished, and the said open fields, half-year lands, shack lands, fens, commons and waste grounds were divided, and specific parts or shares thereof allotted to the several persons interested therein, according to their respective shares, estates, rights and interests in, over, or upon the same.* [12]

Further sections of the Act noted that new ditches could be cut and old ones straightened, for example, the stream at Baconsthorpe. A new pattern of field

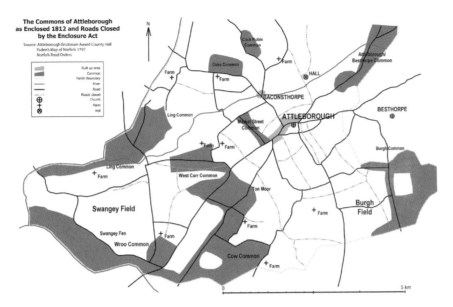

The Commons of Attleborough
as Enclosed 1812 and Roads Closed
by the Enclosure Act
Source: Attleborough Enclosure Award County Hall
Faden's Map of Norfolk 1797
Norfolk Road Orders

A map of the commons shows large areas of common to the west of the town and to its north-east. Market Street common provided an important space at the entrance to the town where stock could be held for the night and could drink at the horse pond.

boundaries and access to new fields was drawn up at the Award and, as the map shows, many of the old service tracks to the open fields were closed. A new simpler road pattern was created. Of course many lost their grazing rights but were compensated with tiny pieces of land often well away from their homes so that they preferred to sell them. In this way the larger landholders tended to become still larger.

Henry Norton is an example of how this worked. He was allotted 28 pieces of land, many of which were tiny. Of these most would have been bought from the smaller landowners. The manorial complexity is revealed in that lands he acquired were allotted to the manors of Mortimer's Millshaw, the rectory of the two parts, Chanticlere's, Buckenham Lathes, Buckenham Close and Buckenham Castle. Henry would therefore have many small quit rents to pay to the various manors and many manor courts to attend. A large allotment of 57 acres was made to the town poor land to provide fuel for the poor and further allotments went to the School Charity and the Town Lands. Fencing, ditching and new roads had to be paid for by those with lands abutting them so that there were considerable costs involved. The landscape of new hawthorn hedges, larger fields and some new farms replaced the last vestiges of the medieval system.

The great road has remained the main thread of the story of Attleborough. The church, once a major element in its history, has become less of a focus though many community activities do still revolve around it and the later Nonconformist churches. Enclosure reorganised the landscape around the town but, because of the railway, industry and new housing have spread a long way into that countryside from the medieval core. Attleborough Hall, the home of manorial lords for many centuries, has somehow remained isolated from all this.

Aylsham chronology

AD 100–400	Brampton Roman pottery centre
	Roman site at Bolwick (excavated in 1950)
	Roman pottery (43 pieces found at 8–12 Red Lion Street in 2003 excavation)
500–800	-ham place name: OE name Ægel(s)ham
800	South Erpingham hundred
800–1000	Late Saxon Thetford ware (found at 8 to 12 Red Lion Street in 2003 excavation)
1086	Domesday Book: Aylsham a royal manor
	St Michael's Church not in Domesday Book
c. 1280	Church arcade
1296	Market charter regranted 1519
1301	References to Aylsham linen and worsted, Aylsham mercers and weavers in London and Norwich
1327	Robert Poley appointed ulnager for hemp and linen cloth in Norfolk
c. 1380	The church tower arch and various windows
1467	Robert Toppes, merchant of Norwich, leaves money to church and poor
1488	Church porch given by Richard Howard, Sheriff of Norwich
1611	Bishop Jegon buys Manor House
1616	Sir Henry Hobart buys the manor of Blickling and builds the Hall
1617	Bishop Jegon's monument in the church
1618	Sir Henry buys the manor of Aylsham Lancaster
1624	Aylsham Rental of Aylsham Lancaster. Much building around Market Place
c. 1700–1800	Many new brick buildings in Aylsham
1770s	The Bure Navigation constructed
1790	Emmanuel Baptist Church built
1794	The Norwich–Aylsham–Cromer turnpike
1880s	Midland and Great Northern station
	Norwich–County School station
1912	The great flood
1939–45	Oulton airfield constructed
1970	The Aylsham bypass

Bishop John Jegon's monument in Aylsham church.

Aylsham

The River Bure rises in the grounds of Melton Constable Hall and its valley opens out into, in Norfolk terms, a considerable feature running broadly south-south-east off the south side of the Cromer Ridge. The wide flood plain sweeps round the promontory of boulder clay upland which provides a suitable site and bridge point for the growth of the town. Important west–east and south–north roads cross to the south of the river. The site, rather like that of Norwich, seems an obvious one for a settlement yet, as at Caistor-by-Norwich, the major nearby Roman settlement was some three miles to the south at Brampton. Was Aylsham already a Celtic settlement? Not according to recent work by the Norfolk Archaeological Unit.[13] However, this excavation of a corner of the market place, though covering only a very small area, revealed evidence of Roman ditches with pottery and tile in them.

After the Romans left Brampton *c.* AD 400 there was an archaeological gap there until the Norman Conquest. Yet by 1066 Aylsham was held as a major manor

The focal points of Aylsham are the market place and the church and they are set on the highest point of the headland. The slope away to the north, north-east and east means that the church stands out well in the area. (Photograph taken in 1981.)

of Gyrth Godwinson, Earl of East Anglia, and it was a large holding. It consisted of 16 carucates (1,920 acres) of land, 20 villagers, 88 smallholders, two mills and woodland for 400 pigs. This was an important holding and must have evolved over some length of time. The -ham place name argues for an early Saxon settlement; perhaps it is not too fanciful to date it from *c.* 600. Why should a Roman town at Brampton have not continued? The Roman demand for pottery obviously ceased and a new east–west route replaced the earlier Roman road. The small Roman town lost its *raison d'être*, perhaps Brampton (the 'burnt town') was an unattractive site of derelict pottery kilns. The new settlement had a spread of field land round it on the fertile loams and watermills on the River Bure.

The excavation in 2003 revealed evidence of the earliest buildings in Aylsham as between *c.* 1100 and 1300; pits, postholes and pottery revealed that timber structures long preceded any of brick on that site. These would be contemporary with the early days of the market (1274–75) and the building of the splendid parish church.

Aylsham's manors

Aylsham, like so many of Norfolk's towns and villages, was divided into several manors. The manor of Aylsham Lancaster was the largest, as revealed in the 1624 rental.[14] This was a part of the Duchy of Lancaster lands and in 1401 became

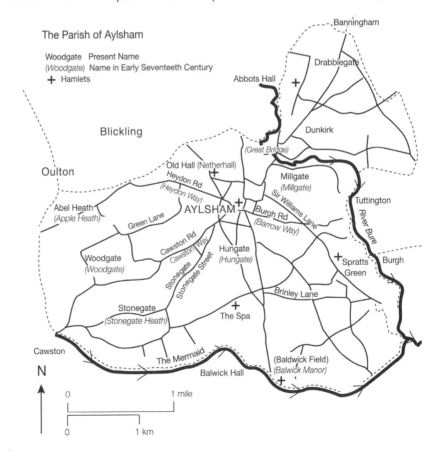

The Parish of Aylsham

Woodgate   Present Name
(*Woodgate*) Name in Early Seventeeth Century
+ Hamlets

the capital manor for the Duchy lands in Norfolk, Suffolk and Cambridgeshire. There were three other manors in Aylsham, those of the Vicarage, Sexton's (Woods) and Bolwick.

Extracts from the Court Book of Bolwick Hall for 1654 show that Robert Jegon, Bishop Jegon's son, surrendered lands of the manor in Marsham and this underlines how manorial lands often disregarded parish boundaries in Norfolk as is shown on the map of Sexton's manor.

LEFT: *The manor of Aylsham Wood (formerly Sexton's) included property in six townships outside Aylsham itself.*

This shows the lands based on a custumal of 1542 and shows how far the manor spread into seven neighbouring parishes.[15] There are also many references to lands in Sexton's Field on the north side of the river. There are also references to tenements in Millgate Street and on the south side of the great bridge.[16]

These references suggest that the Millgate part of Aylsham was not all in the hands of the Manor of Lancaster. However, Aylsham Lancaster did occupy most of the town including the market place. An article by Joan Turville Petre on the tofts of Aylsham Manors throws some light on the relative sizes of the four manors.[17] As the author says, the term *toft* 'designates a portion of land assigned to a named tenant'. In the Manor of Aylsham Wood (formerly Sexton's), there were 44 tofts in seven townships (six of them outside the Parish of Aylsham); in Aylsham Lancaster 62 tofts were named in the court rolls (1462–1582) and in Aylsham Vicarage 19 tofts were named between 1641 and 1699. Interestingly Turville Petre found no mention of tofts in the Manor of Aylsham Bolwick. She noted that some tofts were split between the manors and that they may have pre-dated the subdivision of the original great manor. A total of 100 tofts is listed for the parish of Aylsham whereas in 1086 there were 122 property occupiers. The complexity and number of these units suggests

BELOW: *The 1624 rental makes it possible to plot the market stalls that then existed. (See page 30.)*

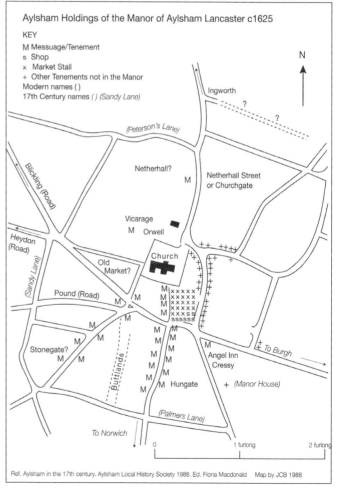

that Aylsham had a considerable population of tenants farming their land well before 1066.

The tofts were not coherent units of land; they may have consisted of a house and pieces of land in several places which became known by the name of a particular person. Later pieces of land could be referred to as being of that holding as a means of reference. Finally Turville Petre suggests that a proportion of the tofts had names of Scandinavian origin, which is not surprising in this part of East Anglia.

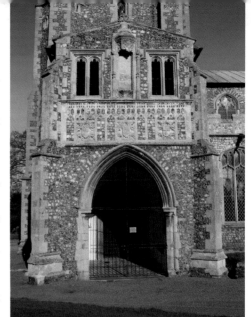

The outstanding porch of Aylsham's church was the gift of Richard Howard in 1480.

The town

Which is the earlier, church or market? There must have been a Norman church yet none is mentioned in Domesday. As already suggested the fact that the town was an important centre of the Duchy of Lancaster holdings in Norfolk has almost certainly been significant. Blomefield states that 'this noble pile was built by John of Gaunt' (1340–99); Pevsner and Wilson do not mention this. Cotton and Catter-mole note several other bequests to 'reparations'.[18] These suggest a prosperous period in the town's history of the mid-15th century, perhaps because of the worsted trade.

The worsted industry and before that the manufacture of linen were important elements in the prosperity of Aylsham and its neighbours from 1301.[19] Before the Black Death of 1349 the two best known fabrics produced in north east Norfolk were known as aylshams (linens) and worsteds (woollens). A steady flow of aylsham cloths, worsted cloths and coverlets of worsted was reaching Oxford

The Textile Producing Area of Norfolk before 1350.

Source Sutton NA XL Pt III

N

Field Dalling

HOLT

NORTH ERPINGHAM

NORTH GREENHOE

Corpusty

SOUTH ERPINGHAM

North Walsham

TUNSTEAD

Honing

HAPPING

EYNSFORD

Wood Dalling

Salle

Aylsham

Worstead

Dilham

Foulsham

Scottow

Sloley

North Elmham

Reepham

Cawston

Lammas

Tunstead

LAUNDITCH

Elsing

TAVERHAM

Catton

Norwich

Places underlined known to produce textiles before 1350
Places in italics have mercers' surnames mentioned in the text
HUNDREDS

The north-eastern quarter of Norfolk produced many named cloths before 1350.

by 1301. In 1332 Richard Elsing was paying seven shillings for pieces of white aylsham linen. It is suggested that Aylsham, like Norwich, was the centre for the finishing trade and that 'sophisticated napery' was spun from flax and coarse linen from hemp. By 1345 so much linen was being made in Norfolk as to merit the appointment of an ulnager (quality controller). In the same period worsted cloth was also important; Richard Elsing had a 'robe drop de raie de worstate' (striped) in his inventory. Worsted was also used for furnishing, and some was known as 'Dilham say' (serge or worsted). Elsing also had worsted beds and the Great Wardrobe had a bed of twelve pieces costing £16 with a cover and tapet (curtain) of blue worsted.

Many London mercers had names showing that they originated from this area. Sutton quotes Ekwall's work on mercers' names and points out that by 1270 to 1360 five hundred emigrants to London carried names revealing their Norfolk origin.[20] He found 41 Norfolk places as origins for surnames – there were mercers from Aylsham, Cawston, Corpusty and Lammas (all in the hundred of South Erpingham) and more still from Eynsford hundred. Initially mercers dealt with linen goods but gradually worsteds became part of their trade. Sutton argues that 'there is really not much doubt that (the Norfolk linen industry) was located in the area north of Norwich around Aylsham'. The variety of wool and cloth types made the task of an ulnager difficult and attempts to apply controls to cloth sizes and quality failed. High quality linens from Flanders gradually reduced the Aylsham market but worsteds competed successfully until the New Fabrics (Norwich stuffs) raised the quality of the cloth produced and led to a concentration in Norwich. The wealth from these two types of cloth contributed both to the building of many new houses and the rebuilding of many of the churches of north-east Norfolk.

The sequence of Aylsham church's surviving parts is given by Pevsner and Wilson as that of a 13th-century nave and aisles, Decorated tower arch and tower and chancel east window. The transepts are dated to 1377 – in the Perpendicular style, as are the chancel chapels.

*The Black Boys inn
dominates the south-west
corner of the market, having
undergone several alterations
– until the 1930s, the centre
bay gave open access for
carriages to the rear yard.*

*Behind the mainly brick
façades around the market
place lie a number of
timber-framed buildings, for
example the stationer's and
number 18 Red Lion Street.
Several of the buildings on
the west side of the market
are also timber framed.*

The main south to north road through Aylsham skirts the east side of the churchyard and the market lies almost due south of it. Sixteenth-century references in Aylsham Lancaster court books refer to 'lately built' and to cellars in buildings around the market place. As the market dates at least from 1296 we can picture a number of timber framed open hall buildings around it, some with shop fronts very similar to modern Lavenham. Certainly by the 16th century they were being modified by floor insertions, chimney stack insertions or complete rebuilding. Timber was in good supply in the area, at least in 1086. As late as the 1624 rental, market stalls were still an essential element of the market. A small town hall was built in 1856–57 as Aylsham began to assume the functions of a 19th-century country town. The union workhouse built in 1848–49 (later St Michael's Hospital) again emphasised this role but it was placed outside the town and now

*Hungate (*LEFT*), the original Norwich Road, has several timber framed buildings along it, as also have Red Lion Street and White Hart Street.*

BELOW: *Aylsham market place and surrounding area, redrawn from tithe map 303 in the Norfolk Record Office.*

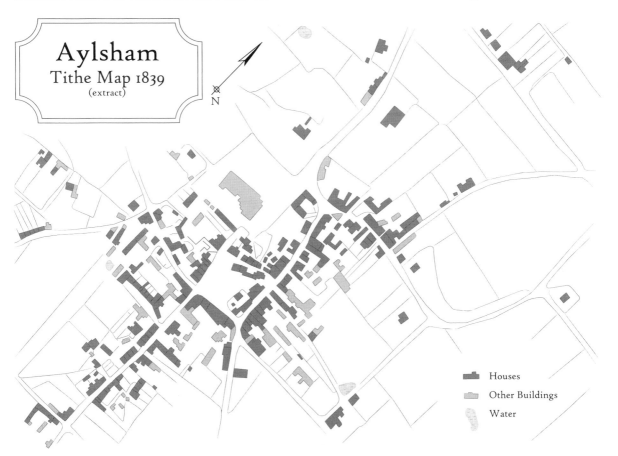

Aylsham
Tithe Map 1839
(extract)

N

Houses

Other Buildings

Water

it is undergoing renovation as part of a new estate. Outside the core of the town, on the Blickling Road, Aylsham Old Hall was built in 1686 as a dower house for Blickling Hall.

To find a full description of a town prior to the tithe map and its schedule is a bonus for any historian. In Aylsham's case a rental of the Manor of Aylsham Lancaster was drawn up *c.* 1624 which described the properties belonging to the major part of the parish.[21] This rental, transcribed by members of the Aylsham Local History Society, is a valuable source for the study of the town in the seventeenth century. Its value is enhanced by the detail which it gives about properties, market stalls and the number of bays of which buildings were constructed for example, so we can construct a map to show the town's layout (see page 25). Sir Charles Cornwallis, who had married Bishop Jegon's widow and was lord of the manor in 1624, held

> *capital messuage cont. 10 spac (bays)*
> *a barn 8 spac. a gatehouse and*
> *other buildings 17 spac. with*
> *stables 7 spac. and le*
> *woodhouse 2 spac. and 3 yarde*
> *orchard garden and le hopyard*

Robert Reyner had held a property in the market place *since the 21 December 1590 a mess. 4 spac. a shop 1 spac.* The former is almost certainly what is still known as the Manor House on the Norwich Road and the latter one of the buildings edging the market place.

In 1616 Sir Henry Hobart, Lord Chief Justice, bought the Blickling estate from Sir Edward Clere. Previously there was a moated house, built in the 1390s, which had been added to by the Boleyn family. The Hobart purchase marked the rebuilding of Blickling Hall but also the acquisition of a large estate which included the manor of Aylsham Lancaster as well as many others including Cawston and much of Wymondham. This great estate and its demands for supplies must have had a considerable impact on Aylsham after 1616. The building of Aylsham Old Hall and its barns in 1686 as a dower house for Blickling is one example of the visible impact of this connection.

Several fine 18th-century Aylsham buildings probably owe their existence to their providing residences for lawyers, physicians and superior shops to deal with the demands of Blickling Hall and its estate. Bayfield House (1 White Lion Street) dates from the 1740s.

Was 1639 an important year for St Michael's church in Aylsham or an ordinary one? This question is asked because an excellent set of churchwardens' accounts, kept by Christopher Sankey and John Durrant, exist for that year.[22] The large quantities of brick and 'stone' being used may have been for the churchyard walls rather than the church but they underline the work involved in maintaining the church and the links created with the surrounding area. It is assumed that 'stone from Cromer' is beach flint although it could possibly be limestone shipped in from Barnack. The extracts given below for the 1639 November account give some idea of the concerns of the Aylsham churchwardens in that year: most of them seem to be with building and repair work. We have a picture of stone-laden carts in a continuous stream on the road from Cromer to Aylsham; the last hill up from the bridge must have tested horses and carts to the full.

> Item to Mr John Neave for fetching of bricke from Tottintowne [Tottington] and one loade of stone from Cromer 11s.
> To the said Allen for one loade of stone fetching from Cromer 6s.
> One load of stone fetching from Cromer by Robert Burre 6s.
> To Widow Swifte for feaching one load of stone from Cromer 6s.
> . . . To Thomas Clare for bread and beare to the labourers that wrought in the churchyarde at times 4s.

Millgate, a later part of the town

The name Millgate speaks for itself. It would seem that perhaps until c. 1750 the watermill was separated from the small town on the hill by open land. In 1524 Robert Jannys, one of the wealthiest men in Norwich, left the mill to the people of Aylsham so that the rent would provide an income for a schoolmaster to teach grammar. Like several other Norfolk towns Aylsham later lost this endowment!

Bure House, opposite the Maltings, was built in 1768.

In 1771 Robert Parmeter bought two properties next to the river in Millgate; they were converted into the Anchor Inn soon afterwards. The inn closed in 1961 and the building became a private house known as Bridge House.

The churchwardens' accounts of 1708–10 show that £13 9s 4d was spent for 'viewing and measuring the river to make it navigable'.[23] This makes it clear that it was not navigable before then; whether Roman pottery had left Brampton by river is an interesting question. The development of Norfolk agriculture in the 18th century may have been a factor in the passing of an Act of Parliament in 1773 to allow the construction of five locks and the digging of new channels in the river to cut off bends. Local landowners took their shares in the project and in 1779, after various mishaps, the Navigation was opened.[24] The wherries were of 16 tons burden and drew three and a half feet (just over a metre) of water. The navigators' toll books list the following goods that were moved by the canal:

D Barley	U Coal	U Fish and Salt	D Flour
D Pollard	U Billet	U Maize	U Seed
D Beans	? Gravel	D Manure	D Malt
D Osiers	? Hay	D Wheat	U Cinders
U Deal timber	? Scales		U Cake
D Marl	D Wool[25]		

(D = Downstream,
U = Upstream)

Agricultural activity dominates the list and underlines the economy of the area. Milling and malting were the major commercial activities. As well as Aylsham at the head of the navigation there were three other mills on this canalised river above Coltishall: at Buxton, Oxnead and Burgh. All this activity led to the growth of

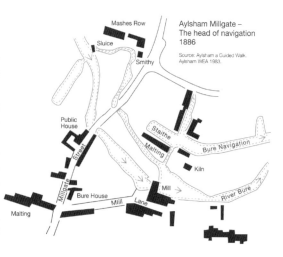

Aylsham Millgate –
The head of navigation
1886

Source: Aylsham a Guided Walk.
Aylsham WEA 1983.

a new canal-side community in Millgate. By 1881 there were 17 watermen, 16 builders and five millers in Millgate; agriculture still employed 40, however.[26] In the 18th century the Parmeter family became the major owners of the property at the head of the navigation and William Parmeter died in 1793. In his will a nice picture of the busy area is given:

> I give and devise all that my messuage and dwelling house wherein I now dwell, together with the malthouses, granaries, houses, outhouses, yards, gardens, orchards, lands and grounds . . . being in Millgate Street in Aylsham . . . to Robert Parmeter, my brother. Also, subject as aforesaid, I give all that my estate and interest and terms of years yet to come and unexpired, of and in, all that staithe, yard, grounds and bank with the warehouses, houses and buildings erected in part of the same situate standing, lying and being next Aylsham Navigation, and also all my subscriptions or shares of £220 lent and advanced on the credit on the tolls of the said Navigation, by the said Robert Parmeter, my father, deceased, and all interest to my brother Robert.[27]

The Parmeters were shareholders in the Navigation for obvious reasons. Aylsham then saw a canal phase in its development until the arrival of the railways in 1881 and 1882 and the flood of 1912 put paid to the canal as an element in its economy.

The railways of Norfolk have a literature all to themselves. Compared with bigger towns, such as Norwich, and more especially the industrial towns of the midlands and the north of England, the arrival of the railways did not lead to any obvious growth in the size of Aylsham. Aylsham lost its railways in the 1960s, apart from the mini line to Wroxham. It was bypassed in the 1970s and it is only since 2000 that any large scale housing development has struck it. Its links to Blickling and the Hobarts saw gracious 18th-century façades cover its earlier timber framed buildings and with its church, market place, mill and handsome brick buildings it remains one of the least changed of the towns discussed in this study.

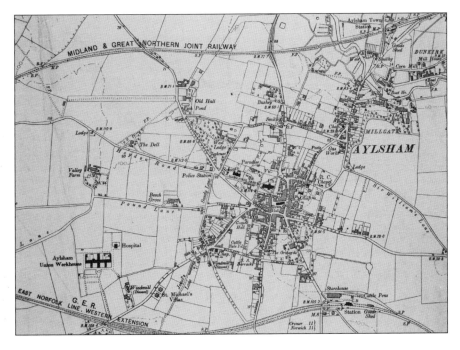

Aylsham had two railway stations, one on the Great Eastern Railway and the other on the Midland and Great Northern joint.

Diss chronology

10,000 BC	Diss Mere forms at the end of the Ice Ages
AD 65–400	Roman occupation, the Stone Road and a town at Scole
400–1000	Anglo-Saxon settlement: many nearby villages in *-ham* and *-ton* place names but Scole, Frenze and Diss all unusual names
800–1000	'Thorpe' and 'by' place name evidence of Danish occupation
1086	Domesday survey; Diss in Suffolk a royal manor and Watlingeseta royal manor in Norfolk
1066–1200	The Norman settlement – New Buckenham and Eye castles
1274–75	Diss market charter
1299	Charter for Diss fair
1290	Earliest elements of the church, tower and nave arcades
1430–40	Additions to the church; aisle windows, new porches
1524	Duke of Norfolk's funeral procession
1546	Thomas, third Duke of Norfolk in the Tower of London
1547	Henry Howard, Earl of Surrey, executed
1600s	Linen manufacture in the Diss region
1769	Norwich to Scole turnpike
1776	Parish workhouse exists
1800	Sale of Simpson's Brewery to Dyson
1801	Population 2,246
1835	Depwade Union workhouse built at Pulham
1845	Linen and malting phase – five maltings in Diss
1846	The Guildhall sold and demolished
1849	London to Norwich railway built
1850	The Sanitary Report for Diss
1851	Population 3,637
1881	Cholera outbreak in Diss
1901	Population 3,745
1951	Population 3,503
2000	Electrification of the Norwich to London railway
2001	Population 6,742

Diss

It is the mere that makes Diss unique amongst Norfolk's market towns. It is five and a half acres in area, its greatest depth is 20 feet (6.1 m), its origin is geological but far from fully explained. The underlying rock is chalk which is porous and within which the water table fluctuates.

Diss lies off the main south–north axis of the Roman Pye Road from Colchester to Caistor St Edmund. The main Roman site near to Diss was at Scole which becomes more important with the discoveries of each excavation in its neighbourhood. Perhaps a river port, it is at a classic bridge point on the River Waveney rather than a crossroad junction. The road west from Scole is only marked as a probable road on the latest edition of the *Historical Atlas of Norfolk* (p. 29), and no road is shown running from Scole to the east. By AD 1000 Diss had replaced Scole as the centre for this section of the Waveney Valley.

OPPOSITE: *The view down St Nicholas Street to the church of St Mary*

BELOW: *The church and town of Diss seen from the mere.*

Diss in its setting: roads splay out to the north of Diss, leading to Shelfanger and Winfarthing, to the Heywood and (to the north-east) to Burston. The main east–west axis is the road from Thetford to Great Yarmouth (now the A1066).

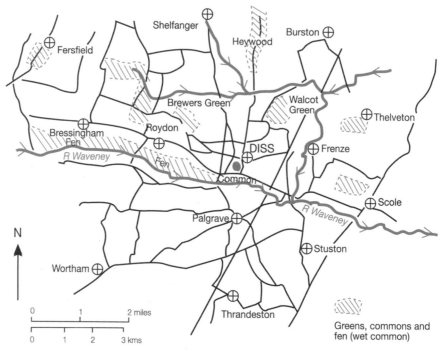

Clusters of timber framed buildings survive in Diss to remind us that it lies in the wood pasture area of the county. They line Mere Street, Market Hill, St Nicholas Street, Mount Street, Church Street and Denmark Street. Another cluster edges Fair Green to the south of the main road by the bridge.

The town is wrapped round and above the mere, its splendid parish church of St Mary providing a key focal point to the north-east of the mere with the Market Street running down the east side of it. Faden showed the east–west road as less direct in 1797 with its western approach leading into the market before following the line of the mere to pick up the valleyside route eastwards. Interestingly, this route was never turnpiked. The railway reached Diss in 1849 and in 1854 it became the Eastern Counties Railway. In contrast with most Norfolk market towns its recent electrification has led to considerable industrial and residential growth of a new Diss.

Modern market traders operate in the shadow of the 15th-century church of St Mary and the timber-framed Dolphin House, built as a merchant's house c. 1520 and used as a pub during the 19th century and into the 1960s.

The most striking surviving buildings are the King's Head in the market place and Dolphin House, a former public house carrying a date of 1520. The Manor House survives in Mount Street and at the junction of the Market Place and St Nicholas Street is a late-15th-century timber building with an angle post with carvings of the annunciation and the nativity. Lacon's old maltings in St Nicholas Street and the malthouse on Fair Green are reminders of the once important brewing and malting industry. The problems of the maintenance of timber framed buildings are well illustrated by the history of the now demolished Guildhall. In 1755 the trustees of the Guildhall, in an agreement of 3rd May, noted:

> *Whereas the southeast corner of the house called The Guildhall is by time and weather considerably impaired so as to be visibly sunk or settled down, and the chamber floor in the same part rotten and broken, to prevent any further damage we consent that John Barnard present tenant or lessee should get the same sufficiently repaired, a new floor laid, the walls daubed or cast, a new ceiling made; and what else may be thought necessary to render the same a safe and warm lodging room.* [28]

ABOVE: *The Saracen's Head in Mount Street (17th century).*

BELOW: *Mount Street, running north from the church.*

BOTTOM: *A Venetian window in Market Hill.*

The Guildhall was called both Guildhall and Town House and in 1738 its abuttals gave the churchyard to the west, a messuage formerly of Samuel Foulser to the east, the highway from Diss market to Dickleburgh to the south and the lands formerly of W. Manning to the north. A lease of 1596 gave exactly the same abuttals as does one of 1623 bearing Blomefield's hot cross bun – his mark which he placed on all documents which he had read!

The parish of Diss stretches well beyond the town – its abuttals are rather odd. The River Waveney forms the southern boundary, that to the west is an arbitrary one with Roydon and that to the east is defined by Frenze Beck for two miles. The northern boundary is curious. It stretches as a tongue known as Heywood between Burston and Gissing to the east and Shelfanger and Winfarthing to the west. This was shown largely as common on Faden's map of 1797 and earlier; as the name suggests, it was probably woodland and it stretched to the Pulham–Buckenham road. The total area of the parish was given by White as 3382 acres in 1845.

Like so many Norfolk parishes Diss had a complicated manorial structure. The manors were those of Diss-cum-Membris, Heywood, Heywood Hall and the Rectory. Diss-cum-Membris overlapped into several parishes:

> *The manor doth extend from the river dividing Suffolk and Norfolk on the south, through a great parte of the town of Diss into Roydon, Burston, Frenze, Shelfanger and Winfarthing. But what other towns we plainly know not and that Thomas Earl of Arundel and Surrey, Earl Marshall of England, hath a manor called Heywood . . . Richard Fisher Gent, a manor called Heywood Hall . . . the manor of Diss Rectory do lie enjoining, bordering or intermixed in amongst or near unto the lands of the manor of Diss.* [29]

The custumal of 1636 explains that fines were arbitrary (i.e. the lord could set them), the eldest son inherited, no heriot (payment of the best beast at death) was known, the hayward took all payments made for failure to carry out agricultural practices properly, the bailiff took the fines paid on property transactions at manorial courts, the lord could take timber off copyhold land but should leave tops, bark etc to the tenant, bailiffs should take only one penny for impounding stock, tenants had the right to take gravel, sand or clay upon the commons and wastes of the manor and make hemp pits for retting hemp on Diss Moor and Cock

Street Green and to dig furze upon Diss Moor. This custumal gives a picture of the way in which the manor was organised but it tells us little of the functions of the town but it continues:

> There is a weekly market every Friday, a fair on the first day of Saints Simon and Jude: the bailiffs were to take 2d for every stall tilted and not tilted one pence.[30] Any selling from houses along Market Street and/or pent houses should pay 4d.

The tithing customs of the parish of Diss provide further light on the nature of its economy.[31] An undated series of questions was put to parishioners in order to clarify arguments about what was titheable in Diss. Richard Fisher, Robert Cooper, Matthew Wilby, Thomas Shreeve, Thomas Aldred and others were asked to seek answers to a series of questions about tithe payments in a dispute with Richard Cooper, parson and defendant. These questions were asked of a series of elderly inhabitants who in theory (memory allowing!) were familiar with the tithing customs of Diss. Blomefield gives the list in full, and the following elements of the agricultural economy stand out:

> Corn is charged for every tenth sheaf
> Peas for every tenth 'stetch' (row?)[32]

A record of Diss tithes and herbage in 1729[33] gives some details of the crops on which people were paying tithe: the widow Greengrass paid £1 15s for barley and oats, William Chapman £3 for barley and peas and Robert Chilver £2 10s for wheat, barley and hemp. By 1740 the tithe total was £220 18s 6d; this would provide a nice rectorial income at that date. Some tithe payments were still being paid in kind: Mr Burton provided a goose worth a shilling, 20 bales of hay worth £1 10s and, in money, £2. Robert Ayton had to pay six bushels of wheat and two coombs of peas. William Burton had two cows, four acres of wheat, one and a half acres of oats, plus more oats on Shelfanger Road, five acres of barley, half an acre of roots, 15 acres of meadow, a hempland, a further 14 acres unspecified and an orchard and a garden. This came to 45 acres in all for which he had to pay £4 19s 3d in tithe.

The building on the left with the classical portico is the 1854 Corn Hall, a reminder of the importance of cereals in the economy of Diss. Next to it the Greyhound pub occupies a building that dates back to c. 1580; Simon Knott has suggested that the stepped gable and low brick porch could be remnants reused from the lost chapel of St Nicholas, of which Blomefield (vol. 1, pp. 32–3) gives a detailed account.

Oats, wheat and barley were all being grown in 1729, peas and hemp also featured and the cutting of meadow land for hay. No sheep were mentioned but the overall picture is of mixed farming with cattle plus cereal crops, the balance of which is not easy to distinguish, peas, hemp and meadowland were also important. The tithe map land categories listed a hundred years later suggest that cereal growing had been somewhat reduced and grazing increased.

Diss amenities

The problem of repairing the Guildhall has already been mentioned. A well preserved set of Guildhall accounts from 1780 to 1846 underlines that repairs were still often needed.[34] On 6th May 1780 the Trustees of the Guildhall met at the King's Head Inn and because it had been in bad repair they each loaned £10 and Thomas Fulcher £100 to pay the resulting bill which was for £367. Thomas Gilbert, the tenant in 1780, ran a school to teach English language, writing and arithmetic and because of repairs he had had the Guildhall rent free but from 1780 he paid a rent of £10 per annum. By 1794 Reverend S. Westley was paying £15 a year. The Trustees received a valuable income from an estate of 97 acres in Framlingham that had been given to Diss and which produced a rent of £100 per annum. The accounts record that in 1848 the Guildhall was conveyed to the Church Commissioners for £57 19s and was then demolished. In 1908 Kelly's Directory noted that the Framlingham income was divided between the church and the urban district council. After 1809 the accounts broaden out into town accounts when the Trustees paid £1,200 for paving the town and they borrowed £600 interest free from one individual towards this.

Amongst the parish papers is a sad little collection of inventories of Diss paupers and of Diss men who were in Norwich Castle prison.[35] In 1696, for example, John Goodenham's possessions were valued at £2 12s 6d and the cost of his burial 19s of which the coffin cost 5s, the sexton 10d and the woollens to wrap him in 1s 8d. Amongst his possessions were a flock and feather bed with a flock bolster, a feather bolster, a pillow and a coverlet blanket, together worth £1 5s, and a 'chist and a coffer' worth 5s each.

Within the churchwardens' accounts is a single sheet of the Constable's accounts of the October to December quarter for 1836.[36] The constable was a manorial or parish post depending on the balance of local authority. Samuel Cobb was Town Constable and he had to deal with billeting 'large numbers of men and horses' (presumably soldiers) between 10th and 14th October and impressing wagons for them to travel to Norwich and then Ipswich. Why these movements were taking place is not clear. His normal duty on 8th and 9th November was keeping the peace at the fair, for which he was paid 5s, and on 13 Sundays he visited public houses and was paid 13s. He also dealt with a number of vagabonds.

The Church and Dissenters

An interesting result of some tensions between the church and dissenters in Diss was a pamphlet published in 1859. The churchwardens of Diss complained that the ten Trustees proposing a revised charity scheme were all dissenters aiming 'to secure to the dissenting body almost the entire control of the Charities (a problem also met in East Dereham), and we submit that such a practical appointment would be most undesirable'.

The pamphlet reprinted Blomefield's account of the Diss Charities and it made reference to the income from the Framlingham Estates of 93 acres yielding £240 a year and to:

Bell Acre (no detail)	
Chapman's Charity	*Yields 20s.*
Girling's Charity	*Yields 11s.*
Carnell's Charity	*Yields 25s.*
Burton's Charity	*Included Hingall's Wood of six acres, rental to 12 working men*
Cock Street in Fairstead Green	*Free grazing for horses of the poor and for recreation*
Cock Street Fen	*Four and a half acres for firing – by 1859 a rental of £9*
Sand and Gravel Pit	*One acre let*
Mere's Mouth	*Let in two pieces*
The new almshouses	*13 rooms occupied – no endowments*
Hopper House	*One acre – being repaired in 1859*
Messuages etc. in Cock Street including the Guildhall and almshouses	
Walcot Pightle	*4 acres – let to eight poor men*
Gravel Pit field	*Let at £6 10s.*

The pamphlet noted that no church rates had been levied in Diss and that the dissenters wished for a new distribution by the Trustees instead of the funds just going to the churchwardens. It was proposed that one fifth of the income should go to Diss National School and one fifth to the British School which, being Non-conformist, was what probably annoyed the churchwardens.

Enclosed with this charity pamphlet was a separate sheet from the Diss Charitable Fund for March 1832 drawing attention to the fact that 300 families had received soup and coals and that 100 quilts and 181 blankets had been distributed to the most needy in the past winter. There was even a row in January 1832 when Samuel Farrow had ordered beef for the charity soup from Mr Browning rather than from Luccock and Tyrrel because the meat was cheaper. They responded that:

Instead of good fat meat of the best quality, there had been sent in young thin beef; and once or twice beef of a very inferior quality which had been returned.

These letters were printed for the town's readership.

Linen manufacture

The Waveney Valley, on both its Norfolk and Suffolk sides, was important for the weaving of linen. The tithing customs already referred to for Diss show that hemp was one of the titheable crops grown in the area and references to retting pits on the commons show that hemp processing took place locally.

A Tudor ruling that one acre of hemp should be grown on every holding of 60 acres or more was passed to encourage its growth. It is a very demanding crop and

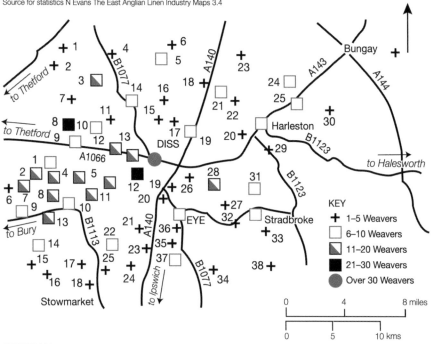

Source for statistics N Evans The East Anglian Linen Industry Maps 3.4

KEY
+ 1–5 Weavers
□ 6–10 Weavers
◨ 11–20 Weavers
■ 21–30 Weavers
● Over 30 Weavers

0   4   8 miles
0   5   10 kms

L:inen weavers in the Waveney valley, showing the number of weavers' inventories listed in the Norwich Consistory Court and the four Archddeaconry Courts between 1550 and 1850.[37]

NORFOLK

1. Eccles 2. Wilby 3. Banham 4. New Buckenham 5. Tibenham 6. Aslacton 7.Kenninghall 8. North Lopham 9. South Lopham 10. Fersfield 11. Shelfanger 12. Bressingham 13. Roydon 14. Winfarthing 15. Burston 16. Gissing 17. Shimpling 18.Tivetshall 19. Dickleburgh 20. Needham 21. Pulham Market 22. Pulham St Mary 23. Hempnall 24. Albergh 25. Wortwell

hemplands occur in many lists of land holdings in the area. Arthur Young, writing in 1804, noted that:

> *This culture in the vicinity of Diss has greatly declined; there is scarcely one tenth grown of what there was sown years past: this is chiefly attributed to the high price of wheat.*[38]

Young noted that spinners could earn from 4d to 8d a day and that most of the cottages in the vicinity had a patch of hemp which helped them as it was profitable and gave the families work. He suggested that government support would be a very good thing for the poor and would give them a better return than potatoes. He argued that one rood of hemp would pay their rent. William Marshall disagreed with Young and suggested national hemp markets with a fixed price would be preferable.[39]

Brewing

As well as being an important centre for hemp growing and linen production Diss was also a maltings and brewing centre. Three breweries operated there in the early 1800s and White listed four in 1845. An extensive collection of papers relating to the purchase of Diss brewery in 1800 by John Dyson of Gunton in Suffolk, gent., from W. W. Simpson provides a remarkable amount of information about the scale and technologies of the brewing trade at the beginning of the 19th century.

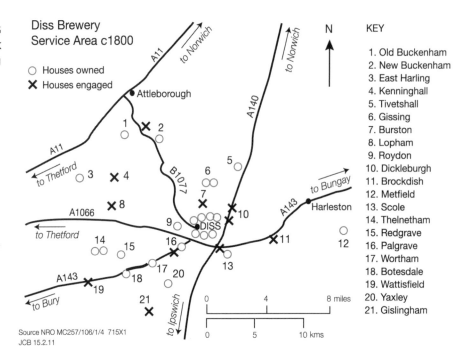

Diss Brewery
Service Area c1800

○ Houses owned
✕ Houses engaged

KEY

1. Old Buckenham
2. New Buckenham
3. East Harling
4. Kenninghall
5. Tivetshall
6. Gissing
7. Burston
8. Lopham
9. Roydon
10. Dickleburgh
11. Brockdish
12. Metfield
13. Scole
14. Thelnetham
15. Redgrave
16. Palgrave
17. Wortham
18. Botesdale
19. Wattisfield
20. Yaxley
21. Gislingham

Source NRO MC257/106/1/4 715X1
JCB 15.2.11

Some 23 public houses were owned by the Diss Brewery and 16 more had agreements to take its beer. The supply routes along the major roads show up quite clearly and illustrate how the Waveney Valley was a focus for this brewery.

First of all it shows how carefully some business accounts were kept. The brewery premises in Diss and 23 public houses were worth £15,900. The accounts showed the details for October 1799 to October 1800 for the malt and hops consumed in 66 brewings:

	£
Malt	3425
Hops	786
Coals	112
Servant wages	67
Six horses	187
Expenses camping out	22
Coopering and wear and tear of barrels	21
Shoeing and tramping of horses	13
Wear and tear on wagons, drays and harness	8
Wear and tear on brewhouse	8
Repairs of premises	100
Duty on 66 brewings at 40 barrels per brewing	790
Expenses, markets, clubs etc.	20
	———
Total	5580 *approx*
Profit on trade at £2.7s. per barrel	574
	———
Total	6154 *approx* [40]

This scale of business, not large by Norwich or Bury standards, was an important industry in the Diss economy. In addition, the brewery had its network of public and north Suffolk.

An inventory for the brewhouse merits full publication elsewhere but major items included:

> One brewing copper as it hangs with the staging doors, irons, barrs, slice put up new in 1771 . . . one mash vat and underback (very bad) . . . one malt kin with a pair of capital Cologne stones . . . one hop net with the tackle thereunto belonging . . . in the malthouse chamber a malt screen, a bushel . . . 36 broad wheel trolleys . . . at the bowling green one large garden rowl, 30 pairs of bowls and jacks.

The total value listed on four pages of details was £2,844 16s.[41]

A proposed navigation

Diss lies on the north bank of the river Waveney and the rivers Little Ouse and the Waveney rise almost back to back in the marshy area beneath a bridge between South Lopham and Redgrave. This almost continuous watercourse led to early schemes for the establishment of a navigable water route in 1656 when F. Mathew proposed such a route to Oliver Cromwell. A number of other proposals to link major towns of south Norfolk and east Suffolk were also made. In 1818 there was a proposal to link Diss and Bungay by a joint navigation. As the first two paragraphs of the prospectus state:

> This navigation will connect a large district of Norfolk and Suffolk with the port of Yarmouth and will be the conduit to transporting the whole surplus produce of the neighbourhood at about a moiety of the present price by land carriage.

> The hundreds of Diss, Guiltcross, Hoxne and Hartismere, will, by its means, find various markets for their produce and trade, and will become, for the first time, directly connected with a large sea-port, to and from which there is an extensive foreign trade, and whence there are ships constantly sailing for Scotland, Newcastle, Sunderland, Hull, Liverpool, London and other places independently of regular traders for the import and export of all kinds of goods and merchandise. They will also, by this navigation, receive that large and cheap supply of coal, which the present limited and expensive land carriage renders it impossible to the poorer, and burdensome to the richer, inhabitants of these districts to obtain.[42]

It was argued in addition that marl at Scole and Frenze and oak timber would also be more easily moved by water. The lack of suitable geology and gradients for storage reservoirs proved a major limitation.

This all came to nothing and Diss has never had a water link westward down the Little Ouse or eastward down the Waveney. In 1849 the arrival of the railway eliminated any such schemes but it did not solve the problem of an east–west link.

Downham Market chronology

c. 10,000 BC	The Fen embayment begins to silt up with land and sea derived sediments
c. 500 BC–AD 43	Iron Age wealth in north-west Norfolk, coin hoards, gold torcs and the Snettisham hoard
c. 43–400	The Roman Fen Causeway from Water Newton (Durobrivae) to Denver and on to Caister-by-Yarmouth
	Further rise in sea level, Roman deposits drowned
400–800	Anglo-Saxon settlement, a key site at Hay Green, Terrington, and later sites on the marshland silts and the fen edge
600	Monastic settlements at Ramsey and West Dereham
1066	Norman Conquest, Castle Rising, Castle Acre and Wormegay Castle
1086	Major landowners in the area are Ramsey Abbey, William de Warenne and Hermer de Ferrers
From 1100	Markets at Downham 1129, West Dereham and Bexwell 1256
1332	59 taxpayers compared with Upwell and Outwell 138
1629	Survey of Downham Market for the Hare family
1630–50	Bedford Levels, Salters Lode and Denver Sluice
1651	St John's Eau and Tong's Drain 1653
From 1750	Turnpike roads built
1801	Enclosure Award. Population 1,512
1836	Union workhouse built
1840	Gas works built
1841	Population 2,953
1847	Ely to King's Lynn railway
1861	County Courthouse built
1871	Paradise Road National School built
1872	National School Board established
1878	Clock tower built
1887	Town Hall built
1894	Urban District Council formed
1896	West Downham civil parish formed
1901	Population 2,472
1911	Population 2,497
1951	Population 2,765
1959	Relief channel to Lynn built
1964	Cut off channel from Hockwold to Denver dug
1992	Electrification of the railway
1990s	Eastern and southern bypasses cut
2001	Population 6,730

Downham Market

The marshland fens to the west of Downham have been a scene of changing river courses and frequent floods for many thousands of years. Three critical events changed the nature of Fenland drainage near to Downham. The first was the linking of the Great Ouse to its new and present outlet at King's Lynn c. 1300. This opened up the whole of the Ouse river system to trade into and out of Lynn from as far as Huntingdon and Cambridge, to the advantage of Downham. Secondly, the nature of Fen farming changed once the land was drained; the making of the two Bedford rivers, Denver Sluice and the washland between them meant that crop farming began gradually to replace that of stock. Windmills, steam pumps and now diesel pumps allowed water to be pumped off the fields and up into the drainage channels. The third great change, further controlling flooding, was the completion of the Cut Off Channel from Hockwold to Denver to gather up land water from the tributaries to the Great Ouse from Suffolk and west Norfolk.

Downham lies between the uplands to the east and the lowlands of the Fens to the west.

Downham is a classic market site. Barley from the uplands met cattle and sheep from the Fens and exchanges between the two took place at the markets which grew up below the edge of the carstone on which the church was so well placed. The name Downham implies an early Saxon settlement on a slope, its market dating from 1129.[43] Like several other towns in this study Downham developed under the wing of an abbey, in this case that of Ramsey, which lay out in the Fens.

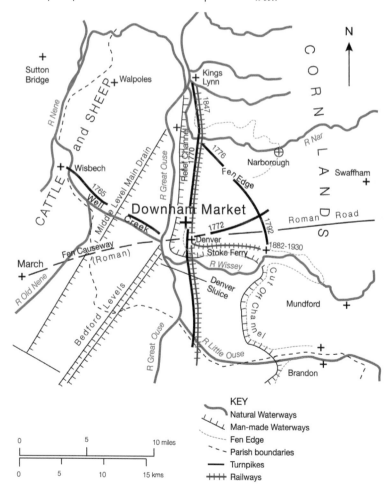

Drainage in the area

Downham lies on the east bank of the Great Ouse. The river was diverted along a cut north of Littleport *c.* 1300 when it gathered up the waters of the Wissey to flow past Downham and on to Lynn. Before 1300 there must have been a river route of some sort, perhaps by the Well Creek, to link Ramsey with Downham in order to move corn, wool and hides between the two. The new channel linked Downham with Ely, Cambridge, Huntingdon, the Little Ouse and the Lark.

The Old Bedford Sluice, Salter's Lode Sluice and Denver Sluice are the key elements in the drainage system of this area. The Old Bedford Sluice controls the outlet of the Old Bedford River, 1636, and Denver Sluice that of the old channel of the Great Ouse which was first built in 1651. The New Bedford River, 1651, remained tidal as far as Erith. As the map shows, later schemes were especially important to Downham. The St John's Eau was cut between the dry land and the Ouse and this sliced the land between Downham and the river into two strips. A second pair of drains, running north east from Nordelph to join the Ouse to the west of Wimbotsham provided the western boundary to the parish of Downham and in 1797 Faden named them as Tong's Drain and Marshland Cut. This area to the west of the Ouse was created as the new civil parish of West Downham in 1896. Because of the drainage schemes it is now an arable area rather than one on which the stock grazed in the dry season.

The parish and manors

Downham was a small parish compared with those of other towns in this study. The dominant manor of the area was that of Wimbotsham which belonged to Ramsey Abbey from pre-Conquest times. This manor came into the hands of the Hare family and a map by Hayward in 1676 which was drawn for Sir John Hare describes the manor site as

> *Enclosed grounds near Wimbotsham church. Sir John Hare. Site of the manor of Wimbotsham with barns, stables, dovehouse and other buildings with the yardes and a long croft adioyning between Downham Lane on the east and Mr Roger Pratt's grounds on the west butting north upon the streete south upon the common pasture (9a – 3r – 20p).*[44]

This manor site later moved to Stow Bardolph and Downham had no main manorial buildings within the parish.

Taxation returns can give some idea of the size of Downham in the 1330s and 1520s. In the early 14th century the Crown established a system of subsidies (taxes) known as the fifteenths and tenths. Many of the returns have survived and those for Norfolk have been edited and published by Timothy Hawes.[45] Downham Market was by no means the most prosperous and populous vill in Clacklose hundred in 1332; it had 59 paying the tax and raising £6 4s whereas Upwell and Outwell had 138, Barton Bendish 115, a surprisingly large number, and Fincham 102. It would seem that by 1332 it was still a relatively unimportant vill in the hundred with Fincham being the most prosperous of the 26. By comparison North Walsham had 207 paying £14 1s 2d and Aylsham 81, paying £10 0s 9d. The wealthiest person in Downham was listed as John de Downham who paid £17 0s 10d. Amongst the taxpayers in Downham were Edmund and John le Barker, Thomas le Fullere, Lawrence atte Market, William and Simon le Miller, Alexander Tailliour, John le Mustard and John le Shephirde, giving a picture of some of the occupations. Others were listed as from Riston, Shipedham, Lingwood and Crimplesham, giving some evidence of the mobility of the population.[46]

In the 1520s during the reign of Henry VIII we were at war with France and there were worries about French and Scottish ships off the Norfolk coast and the need for money for the forces led to a subsidy being imposed on either goods or wages. In Downham 37 men paid tax on their goods and 28 on their wages giving a total of £8 10s 4d; Denver only paid £2 11s 4d. John Rowse Senior paid 26s 8d on his goods and Thomas Cranham 20s. Most paid 6d on their wages and some 4d. We do not know how many avoided taxation but it might be as many again.[47]

The town – the butter market

Downham's early importance as a market appears to have been especially for the summer trade in butter. The firkins could be gathered in from the summer grazings on the Fens and moved by boat to Cambridge and thence to London and it became known as 'Cambridge butter'. An early market seems to have operated at Denver but the collapse of the sluice was used to explain the need for a new butter market; a series of papers in the Hare collection throws some light on this.[48] In 1724 several legal officers were paid a total of £87 8s 2d in order to change the market day. An enquiry was held as to whether a market could be sited on Sir Thomas Hare's land at the Mash

> situated between the River Great Ouse on the west and a certain drain called Downham Drain (otherwise St John's Eau) on the east beginning at a house now inhabited by Richard Cook waterman towards the north and proceeding southward to Denver Gool . . . for buying and selling of butter. And also two fairs to be held every year to be kept at or upon a piece of waste ground . . . belonging to Sir Thomas Hare called the Howdale.

This all took a long time but in the 1740s a petition from Sir Thomas to the King pointed out that

> Large quantities of butter are sent every year from Norfolk to London in firkins for the great benefit of landowners and farmers . . . who make the chief part of their rents by butter and to the great convenience of the cities of London and Westminster who are plentifully supplied with it.

In 1745 a grant with a beautiful royal seal dated 19 Geo. 2 gave the market official status but stated that cattle fairs were also to be held on the Match [*sic*]. The *Universal British Directory* of 1793 commented that firkins of butter contained 56 pounds and that formerly 2,000 firkins a week came to the market but that by the 1790s this had declined to 500 a week. It pointed out that Burleigh's boats left the market at 11 on Monday to reach Cambridge on Tuesday to link up with the wagons. Many wagons were given as leaving the Butter Market daily. Hunt's Upwell boats were also listed. The importance of river traffic for this trade is noticeable. However, by the 1830s Pigot's Commercial Directory noted that the once celebrated Butter Market had moved to Swaffham and in 1845 White's Directory noted that the growing of corn, wool and the feeding of cattle had taken over the emphasis from butter production. This reflects the effects of the draining of much of the former grazing land.

The town – building materials

Carstone is the name given to the crumbly, orangey building stone that provides such a distinctive element to the soil colour and the building fabric of a narrow belt of country stretching from the cliffs at Hunstanton through Downham to Woburn Sands in Bedfordshire. It gives a local character to the Downham buildings. It was used in the building of the parish church and perhaps from 1600 in the rebuilding of the core of the town around the year-long market. It was quarried in the How-dale area to the east of the town and quarries are still worked at Snettisham and Middleton. Various sizes and shapes of stone range from ashlar blocks to much smaller fragments which were edged by brick quoins and window and door frames. In the last 30 years many of the surviving carstone buildings have been cleared to be replaced by the shopping centre. This has diluted what was a distinctive feature of the town and Old Hunstanton and Denver have better examples of carstone buildings which survive. The last large-scale use of carstone in Downham was in the building of the Downham Union workhouse in 1836–37 but even this has now been demolished. The use of brick has been referred to and the later brick buildings of Downham are made from deposits of Kimmeridge clay that conveniently underlie the carstone. Brickyards were worked at Stow Bardolph for many centuries and brick from there was used to build the second court of St John's College in Cambridge in the 1590s; they were still shown on Bryant's map in 1826.

The layout of the town

The main market ran downhill from the crossroads towards the Fen and its western limit, Cow Green, was lined less densely with houses. Along the river bank lay the Hithe or Staithe, from which barges would leave for Lynn or up river; whether the seagoing boats could reach Downham is an open question. In 1629 a survey of the parish was drawn up for John Hare who by then was lord of several manors.[49] John had one messuage, or property; the tenants and other owners had 87 mes-

A striking feature of Downham's plan is that of the two back lanes, Paradise Lane and Parsonage Lane, which give access to the rear of the plots along the main street.

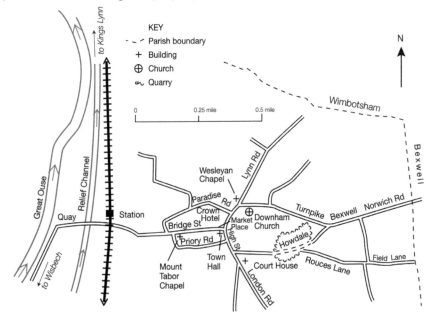

*Building materials and styles
in Downham:*

CLOCKWISE FROM TOP
LEFT: *St Edmund's church:
carstone with ashlar
quoins; the Priory (late
16th century) with its brick
mullioned windows set in a
brick and carstone wall; late
17th-century Dutch gables in
the High Street; the carstone
former malting on the Green
(Railway Road).*

BELOW: *A mixture of
building materials in a
cottage in Bridge Street.*

suages, or tenements, 12 shops and 12 stalls in the market, these holdings totalling
an area of about 800 acres; the common, the Match, between the river and the
town, was another 200 acres.

Thomas Saffrey, Edmund Saffrey, William Say, Thomas Life and Thomas Pigg
all had several holdings. Properties were variously called messuages, tenements
and cottages. Several public houses were listed; the Bull, the Black Swan (probably the present Crown), the Chequers and the Swan. Eight market stalls were
referred as being in The Shambles (the butchery). A Quaker meeting house was
also mentioned. The town was compactly bound between Paradise Lane on the
north, Parsonage Lane to the south and with Cowgate and the market splitting it
neatly into two.

By 1653 a rental of the manor of Stow Bardolph included the names of nine
stall- or shop-holders in Downham Market. There were more stalls than this because William Life held two stalls, three shops and a piece of open ground at the
east end of his shop. Harold Gamble had four shops and William Parlett two. It
would seem from the small rents (varying from 2*d* to 20*d*) that most of the shops
were on the sites of previous stalls.

Two inventories give us some idea of the scale of possessions of local figures in
the 17th and 18th centuries. John Tiffen, a yeoman who died in 1697, left goods to
the value of £235. His house had seven rooms two of which were chambers and in
his parlour chamber were 35 cheeses. He had seven 'burlings', six bullocks, eleven
cows and one bull, eight weanling calves, seven horses and three fillies totalling
£85 but his crops, especially 42 acres of barley valued at £42, beans, wheat and rye

totalled £70. He had a hemp plot and he also had 12 acres of grass and 14 acres of turnips. This is a prosperous yeoman's mixed farm of about 100 acres.[50]

John Bingham was a baker in the town who died in 1771. His property had four chambers, a bakehouse and shop. His style of life was more sophisticated. His inventory included 19 pictures, a weather glass, 12 Delph plates, 24 glasses and two decanters and his plate worth £27 included a sugar dish and cover, a cream jug, a pair of salts, six large spoons and many other small items. In his total valuation of £176, not surprisingly, 14 sacks of flour were worth £22 8s.[51]

The church is of course the oldest building in the town. Full use was made of the carstone and this may have led to the need for more repairs than might have been expected. The original church, perched on the 'cliff', was probably a small towerless building of about 1200 with a transept and tower added c. 1250 and a chancel which was rebuilt much later.[52] In comparison with the great churches of the other market towns, it is less distinguished other than for its superb position. Despite the considerable influence of the Hare family from 1557 in Downham, their remarkable collection of family monuments dating from 1623 is in the Norman church of Stow Bardolph.

The *Universal British Directory* of 1793 gives a list of the principal inhabitants of Downham. It included six attorneys and two surgeons, giving it some status. Those engaged in manufacture include a currier, a wool comber, a stonemason, a skinner, a rope maker, two maltsters, a linen weaver and a bell-founder. A wide range of metal processors, retailers and publicans shows a lively market town in operation. No tanner is listed nor cheese or butter dealer which is surprising.

Downham Market after enclosure; redrawn from the tithe map (DE/TA 9) in the Norfolk Record Office.

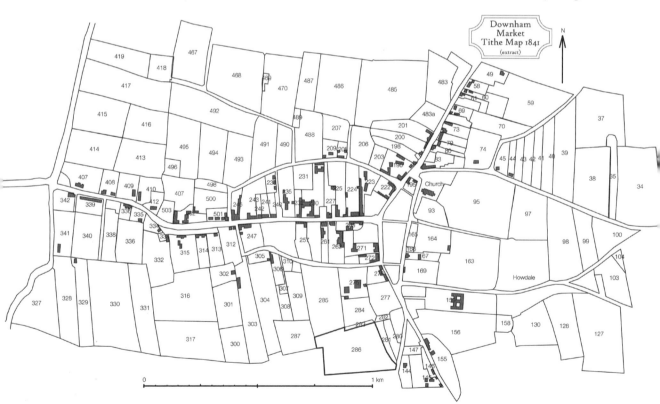

Downham
Market
Tithe Map 1841
(extract)

In 1801 the Downham Enclosure Act was passed. It was an Act for dividing, allotting and enclosing certain open fields and other lands within the several parishes of Downham Market, Wimbotsham and Bexwell. This Act listed 21 pieces of land in various furlongs which are 'intermixed and lie dispersed in small pieces and are very inconveniently situated for occupation and cultivation thereof'. This was the last stage in the removal of the remnants of the medieval open field system that had survived centuries of rationalisation.[53]

The founding of the new Poor Law in 1835 had considerable importance for Downham as the administrative centre of Clacklose hundred. The new Poor Law was centrally and rigorously run by its Commissioners and their records are of great interest.[54] In September 1836 the Workhouse Committee reported on two possible sites, one being the Camping Ground in Wimbotsham and the other, which was chosen, three acres called Workhouse Piece on the lane to the Howdale. The next week the Guardians agreed to accept that Mr Donthorne's square plan at £3,000 be adopted. By November 1837 the Board of Guardians met in the boardroom in the Union workhouse; things had moved fast. The location by the Howdale must have given good access to the carstone with which the new building was made.

The increasing impact of government legislation followed from the Education Act of 1870. A School Board for Downham Market was set up in 1871. It was proposed to add a Board School for 250 children to the National and British School provision for 276 children. HM Inspectors recommended in 1872 that the new school take 350 (the British School was regarded as inefficient) and that new schools be built at Barroway Drove, Salter's Lode, Stowbridge and near Denver church.[55] This second social change about to take place in a primarily agricultural area was bound to create problems for children who regularly helped on the land.

Downham in its setting

The Romans created the earliest west–east route in the area. This took off from the fen at Flag Fen to the east of Peterborough and followed the line of what is now known as the Fen Causeway to the island of March and across to Denver; many Roman finds mark the line of this route. One might logically have expected a market town to have developed at Denver, so why did the Saxons not use such an important site? As with the relationship of Norwich to Caistor St Edmund it seems that a conscious decision was made not to reuse a Roman site.

The south–north road which linked the many prosperous settlements on the fen edge formed the north–south element of the Downham street plan. The market site lies where the later west–east route which used the Well Creek crossed this ancient route. The south–north route has been perpetuated and emphasised by the straightening of what is now the A10 and the building of the railway. Several turnpikes strengthened the importance of Downham. The west–east Wisbech turnpike was made in 1765 and it was continued to Fincham by 1772; strangely the Fincham to Swaffham stretch was not turnpiked but that from Lynn via Swaffham on to Dereham and Norwich had been in 1770. The main south–north road from Cambridge to Ely was renewed by an Act of 1804 to the Chequers Corner in Downham. King's Lynn became the focus for a web of turnpikes which allowed the easier movement of barley to its maltings and for export.

East Dereham chronology

10,000 BC–AD 400	Spong Hill, evidence of Mesolithic, Neolithic, Bronze Age, Iron Age and Romano-British phases
c. AD 600	Spong Hill Anglo-Saxon cemetery
c. 654	Withburga founded a nunnery at Dereham
798	Mention of Dereham in the Anglo-Saxon Chronicle
c. 800	North Elmham cathedral becomes the seat of the bishops of East Anglia
870	Nunnery spoilt by the Danes
970	Dereham and Shipdham given to the Abbey of Ely by King Edgar
974	Abbot Brihtnoth held his first manorial court in Dereham; Withburga's remains taken to Ely
1086	Domesday Book
1169	*Liber Eliensis*
1277	Bishop Balsham's survey of the manor
c. 1540	Dissolution of the Monastery of Ely
1558	Dereham Manor given to the Crown to support the Queen
1581	The great fire; 52 houses burnt
1641	Parliamentary survey of the manor
1679	The second fire; 170 houses at a cost of £19,443
1796	William Cowper came to Dereham, died 1800
1801	Population 2,505
1803	George Borrow born at Dumpling Green, lived there until 1816
1811	Population 2,888
1813	Enclosure Act
1815	Theatre built
1835	Gasworks opened
1846	Railway opened
1850–88	Rev. B. J. Armstrong, Vicar
1851	Population 4,385
1871	Population 5,107
1875	The Queens manor sold to Paine and Brettall of Chertsey
1880	Waterworks opened
1881	Population 5,563
1883	The manor described as lately enfranchised (end of quit rents)
1894	East Dereham Urban District Council established
1901	Population 5,545
1951	Population 6,442
1974	Breckland District Council established
1971	Population 9,384
2001	Population 15,659

East Dereham

East Dereham lies on the plateau between the valleys of the Wensum to the north and that of the Yare to the south. The smaller River Tud forms a southern parish boundary in a shallow valley before crossing Badley Moor to flow eastwards to join the Yare. An even smaller stream rises in Toft Wood to flow through Potters Fen northwards to join the Blackwater and then the Wensum at Worthing. Dereham is at the geographical centre of the county, lying on the boulder clay plateau. Like Swaffham, it has neither castle, abbey nor manor house dominating it; unlike Aylsham and North Walsham it has no significant great estate nearby to have influenced its growth. However, as in North Walsham, a great abbey and later wealthy bishopric has exercised an important influence. In this case it was that of Ely.

The story of St Withburga is one told in many accounts of Dereham. In summary, Withburga was the youngest daughter of Anna, the king of the East Angles (634–54), sister of Etheldreda who founded Ely and Sexburga who also became abbess of Ely. Withburga became a nun and is said to have founded a nunnery

An aerial view of East Dereham, looking west across the market place.

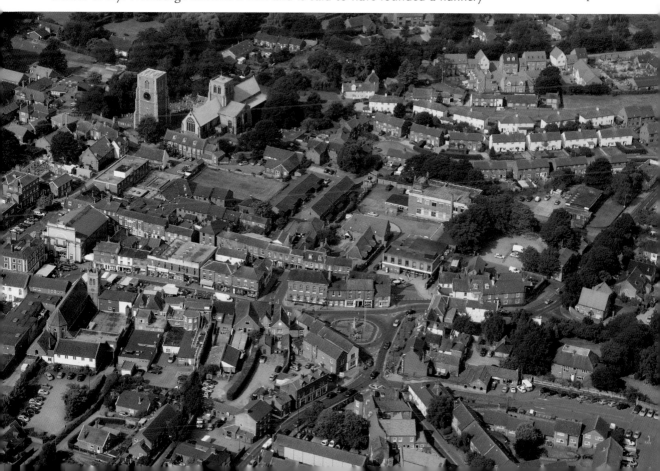

at Dereham in 654.[56] It is by no means certain that the nunnery was on the site of the present church but St Withburga's well is by tradition the site of her shrine. In 974 the monks of Ely moved what was said to have been her perfectly preserved remains to Ely.

Domesday Book does not distinguish between West and East Dereham. However, as there was a famous monastic site in Dereham in west Norfolk near the edge of the Fens the two were early referred to as West and East Dereham to avoid documentary confusion. The Domesday entry for Dereham is under the lordship of the Abbey of St Etheldreda of Ely and it is described as 'always being under Ely',[57] that is, since 1066. Miller suggests that it was in the hands of Ely by 1029 to 1035 and that it came to it 'through the grant of one or other of the old English kings'. Ely was also given a hundred and half of Mitford, giving it various sources of additional income from running the hundred.[58]

Much land in Norfolk was gradually given by the East Anglian kings and later the

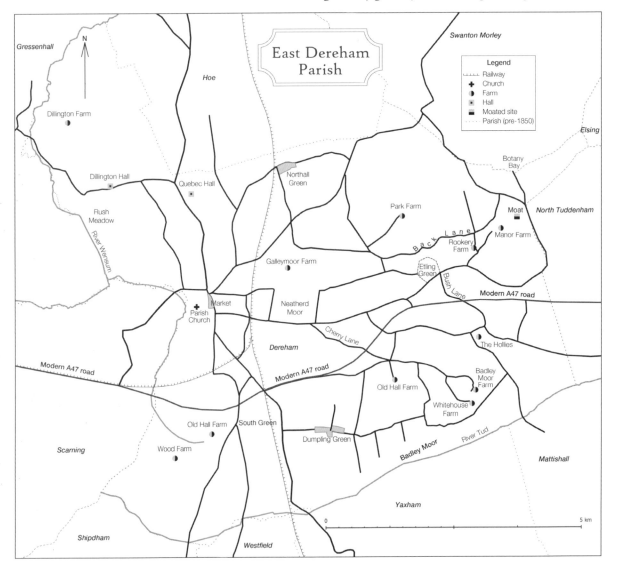

English crown, either to endow new monastic houses or to loyal servants who in turn did so. The bishops of East Anglia had already by 1066 been given estates, for example, at North Elmham and a number of Fenland abbeys had been endowed from the 7th century onwards. Dereham therefore had early protection from Ely and importance to it as a source of foodstuffs and perhaps of timber. In 1109 the bishopric of Ely was carved out of the bishoprics of Norwich and Lincoln and the manor of Dereham and several other Norfolk manors belonging to the abbey were allocated to the estates of the new bishops. The fact that a manor/town was in the hands of a bishop was a major advantage when it came to the development of its market.

The parish of Dereham

The parish is a large one of 5,300 acres. Perhaps from as early as *c*. 1200 until the Black Death of 1349, as the population grew, small secondary settlements developed along the edges of the commons so that Dumpling Green, Toftwood, Etling Green, Northill, Stanton and Dillington became subsidiary hamlets outside the town of Dereham and outside its system of open fields, using the commons for grazing of their stock. The biggest area of common and waste was that of Badley Moor, an area of poorly drained land which remained as an area of inter-common between Dereham and its eastern neighbours until enclosure.

Dereham's main manor descended from the ownership of the Abbey of Ely to the bishops of Ely and then at the Dissolution to the Crown. The Crown allocated it, as with Wymondham, to the support of the Queen, thus it became known as Dereham of the Queen. A second much smaller manor of Old Hall and Syricks or Crekes-together-with-Yaxham was created out of the main manor in the 13th century and Molles manor or Colebornes evolved in the 13th century; it overlapped into Hoe, North Tuddenham and Yaxham. Finally, there was a tiny manor of East Dereham Rectory created by Ely out of the lands belonging to the church, i.e. tenants of the glebe became copyholders. For most purposes it is the great Ely manor with which this account is concerned.

The parish of Dereham was fringed with heaths and commons which survived until they were enclosed in 1818.

The layout of the town

The maps of 1757 and 1815 show the layout of what is now the centre of Dereham but was then the greater part of it. The main axis of the town runs from south to north. The church with its bell tower lies set back from the market place. Boston and Puddy suggest that the original market may have been in Church Street and that the fires of 1581 and 1679 may have led to its repositioning. The churches of both Swaffham and Fakenham are also set back from the markets but not so far as in the case of Dereham.

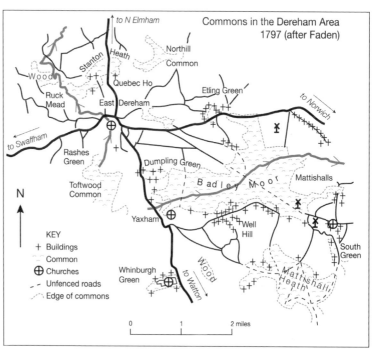

Commons in the Dereham Area 1797 (after Faden)

KEY
+ Buildings
Common
⊕ Churches
- - Unfenced roads
Edge of commons

0   1   2 miles

The enclosure map shows a system of plots running back from the south–north axis on the east side and north–south plots lying south of Church Street. The regularity of these plots might suggest that the settlement was laid out at some early date. The map of 1757 (which forms the frontispiece to Boston and Puddy's book[59]) does not suggest this pattern so clearly but it does show Mr Brown's house which, as Hill House, still dominates the north end of the market place. No map of Dereham exists before that of 1757 but two surveys of Dereham were made, one for Hugh de Balsham, Bishop of Ely, in 1277,[60] the other in 1649 because Dereham was a manor held by the Crown and all Crown lands were revalued by Cromwell's parliament.[61]

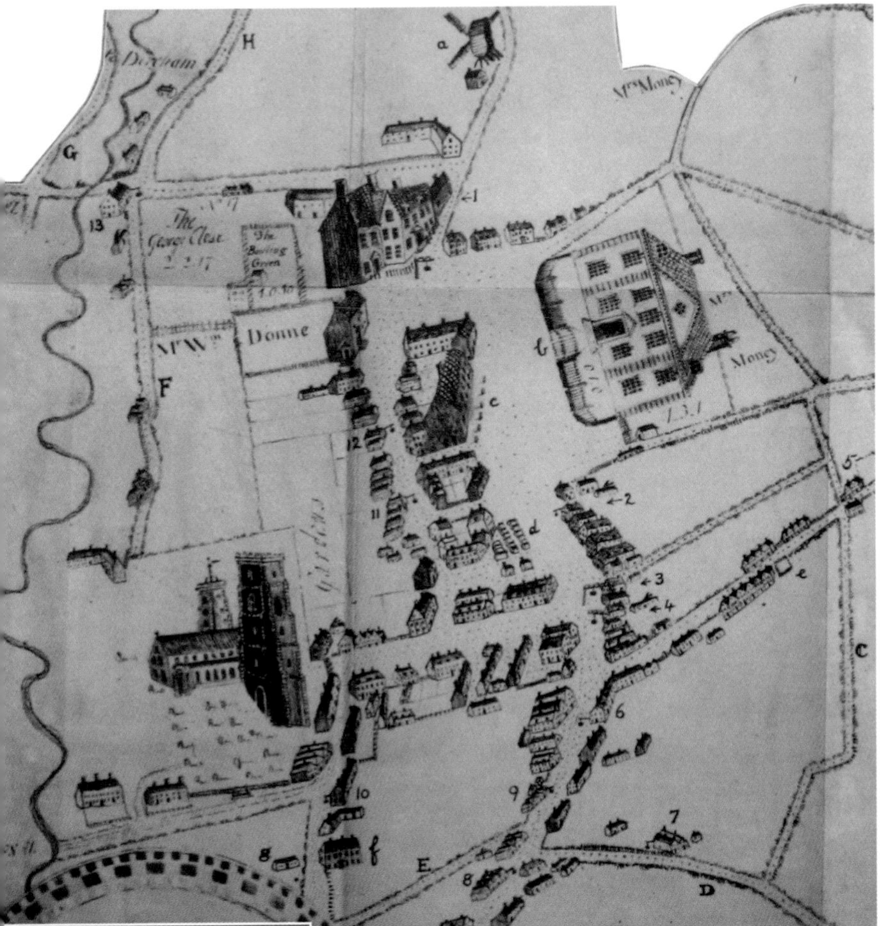

The 1277 survey describes the home farm which kept 10 cows, a free bull, 30 pigs, a free boar and 200 sheep. There were two watermills and a windmill. The market was worth 10 marks and there was a wood of 70 acres called Toftwood, which survived until 1850. The Bishop had a prison for Mitford hundred in the market place because he was also a lord of the hundred and a half of Mitford. Blomefield suggests that a wall of this prison survived as part of a house near the Assembly Rooms in 1746. A vivid picture of the way the manor worked was given by an account of the commons in 1277; for example on Northale Green the town of Dereham and 13 of the homage of William de Stutevile and Thomas de Hereford living near the common intercommoned with the Bishop. On Gallow Tree Moor (the Neatherd) the whole town of Dereham intercommoned with the Bishop. The Bishop had free warren (hunting rights) over the whole manor and he had fisheries at East Mill and Kirk Mill.

Hill House Hotel was built as a private house, mentioned in 1660; its façade was added c. 1740 when it had just been acquired by John Fenn, the antiquary who discovered and edited the Paston letters. It is seen here in a map dated 1757.

After the Dissolution the Bishop's estates came to the Crown and, in the case of East Dereham, remained with it as a property to be held by the Queen. During the Commonwealth, in 1649, parliamentary surveys were made of all royal estates with a view to raising the income from them. Scarlett Neve, gent., appears to have been the tenant of a number of the properties in the centre of the town and the descriptions given of them help to give a picture of Dereham at that date:

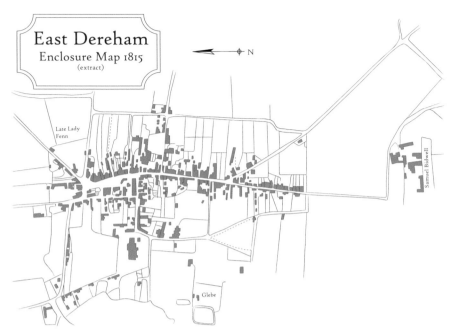

East Dereham
Enclosure Map 1815
(extract)

← ⊕ N

Late Lady
Fenn

Samuel Bidwell

Glebe

LEFT: *East Dereham market place; redrawn from the enclosure map in the Norfolk Record Office (BR90/29/28).*

ABOVE: *The Assembly Room.*

BELOW: *The Guildhall.*

All that decayed ruinous house comonly called or knowne by the name of the Prison House sett, lying and being in the Markett Street of Eastdereham consisting of about six Rooms, with All that house on the East side of it called the Tollhouse, and a small piece of ground sometime a pinfold containing about 13 yards in length and nine yards in bredth and is worth per annum £4.

All those Stalls, Edifices and Buildings sett lying and being in the Markett Place of the Towne of Eastdereham aforesayd . . . worth altogether . . . in words two pound £2.

All those fayres yearely and from tyme to tyme kept at Eastdereham in the county of Norfolk . . . worth per ann ten shillings 10s.[62]

The market place is largely brick built and the Assembly Room of the 18th century and Corn Hall of 1856–57, with its strong columns, are the dominant buildings together with the rather surprising Cowper congregational church, built

LEFT: *Bishop Bonner's cottage is one of the buildings that survived the fires and gives some idea of what pre-fire Dereham must have looked like.*

Small plots, many of them copyhold of Dereham of the Queen, were laid out on a grid that became an area for the building of new cottages rather than, as happened in many other awards, the small plots being bought up by large landowners. The net result of this process was to initiate a new suburb of Dereham, Toftwood, providing a labour force for some of the growing industries in the town.

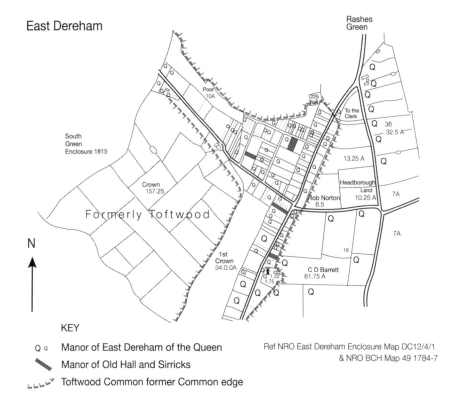

East Dereham

KEY

Q ꟼ   **Manor of East Dereham of the Queen**

◥   **Manor of Old Hall and Sirricks**

ᴸᴸᴸᴸᴸ   **Toftwood Common former Common edge**

Ref NRO East Dereham Enclosure Map DC12/4/1
& NRO BCH Map 49 1784-7

in 1873–74 of Kentish ragstone. Away from the market place some 18th century and early 19th century buildings line Norwich Street and the High Street as far as the dividing point of Baxter Row and Yaxham Road. Church Street leads to the impressive separate bell tower, Bishop Bonner's cottage, now a small museum, and the Guildhall. A mile to the north of the town is Quebec House, built in 1759 by Samuel Rash, a brewer. It is now much added to for its use as a residential home and it lies in its original attractive park which has to some extent been reduced by the addition of a modern estate. To the east of the medieval core of Dereham a 19th century sector evolved around the railways that linked it to Wells and Wymondham in 1849 and Swaffham and Lynn in 1848.

Womack's Green, at the west end of Badley Moor, before enclosure.

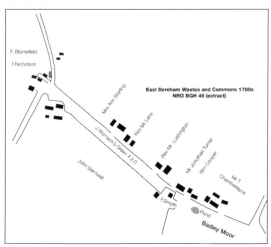

The Enclosure Award for East Dereham of 1815 involved the enclosing of nearly all the commons shown on Faden's map of 1797. New roads were laid out, for example, across Badley Moor to Mattishall, Cut Throat Lane in Yaxham and southwards from Dereham to Shipdham (now the A1075), down the length of South Green and Toftwood Common. Toftwood was the name of the large ancient wood of 157 acres which was still Crown land at the Enclosure. This wood must have been an important asset to the royal manor and before that to the Bishops of Ely. Neither Faden nor the Enclosure Map show it as still being wooded so that either the Crown or a tenant, presumably by permission, had already cleared it. It would be interesting to know what the state of the wood was at the time of its clearance and how much it was worth. There was a windmill and miller's

Inventory

John Gostling the Elder of East Dereham, Currier, 1754

	£	s	d			£	s	d
Cash in the house	5	0	0	**In the leather chamber**				
Wearing apparel	3	3	0	21 dozen & 9 calf skins		52	10	0
Debts in debt book	20	0	0	31 kipps		9	0	0
				3 Soal(?) hides		5	15	0
Kitchen	3	8	0	half a soal hide		0	15	0
				4 hides partly dressed		4	0	0
Pantry								
7 pewter dishes, 12 plates	1	1	6	**In the lumber house**				
				1 butt, 2 rands, 6 shoulders		1	10	0
Little Parlour				11 dozen of lasts at 3s per doz		1	13	0
Two tables	0	14	0	3 cwt of rosin		1	7	0
One bureau and six chairs	1	5	0					
				In the oil house				
In the backhouse				2 cisterns & oil		5	5	0
1 copper as it hangs	1	15	0					
1 mash tub, 1 cooler	0	15	0	**In the shop**				
4 coolers and meat stick(?)	0	7	0	5 hides partly dressed		4	10	0
4 beer vessels	0	6	0	8 calf skins		0	16	0
1 wash tubb	0	6	0	14 skins partly dressed		2	18	0
2 boilers, 1 kittle, 1 skillet	1	6	0					
1 small kittle	0	1	6	**In the shop chamber**				
1 dresser, 1 table	0	5	0	6 hides partly dressed		6	0	0
				12 calf skins		2	2	0
In the cellar				9 kips dressed		1	15	0
3 beer tubs	0	7	0	4 hides & a half		4	0	0
				3 bassel skins & 1 calf skin		0	3	0
In the kitchen chamber				1 skin dressed		0	5	0
1 chest of drawers, 1 table	0	10	0					
1 clothes press	0	10	0					
6 chairs	0	9	0	**TOTAL SUM**		211	0	6
The backhouse chamber								
2 beds	4	0	0					
1 table 4(?) & 15 dozen beer	6	4	0					
thread in the house	2	4	0					
2 beds as they stand	2	2	0					
In the yard								
a parcel of wood	1	5	0					
In the leather house								
2 barrels of pitch	5	0	0					
42 rough hides	42	0	0					
1 horse hide, 2 skins	0	8	0					
11 shoulders	0	16	6					
2 rands	0	18	0					

Some of the words in this inventory are technical terms relating to the leather trade: a **butt** was the thicker or hinder part of a hide or skin; a **shoulder** was a tanned or curried hide, or the part of the hide between the butt and the cheek; a **kip** was the hide of a young or small beast; a **rand** was a strip of leather;[64] **soal** is a variant spelling of 'sole'.

Many fascinating inventories of 17th century Dereham craftsmen have survived and that of John Gostling the elder, currier, is one example.[63] It shows how a town craftsman relied on the mixed farms of the Dereham area for cattle and horse hides to supply his business. As a currier he bought the hides from a tanner. Shoemakers, harness makers and many other craftsmen would have depended on John Gostling for their supply of leather.

house at the south end of the common which had projected into it. It was also in the Queen's manor.

The only common not enclosed was Neatherd Moor. There had been many disputes as to whose stock could graze on it but the Award made it clear that every inhabitant of every ancient messuage or cottage within the parish was entitled to put two milch cows and one heifer or follower on the common every day from 11th May until the following 5th April. The commoners were to elect two herdsmen to keep the cattle off it from 5th April to 11th May to let the grass recover. In 1910 a new scheme for its use was agreed whereby it has become a public park allowing access to all parts of the common and the privilege of playing games on it.[65] As times have changed so the need for grazing for cattle has given way to that for people and their children to have access to a public open space.

A surviving 17th-century building north of the church.

The parish church of St Nicholas

Nothing survives to give any evidence of a church from before the Conquest. Surviving remnants of Norman work led Pevsner and Wilson to suggest that a Norman central tower, one bay to the east of the present tower, fell and damaged the eastern part of the arcades and was replaced by a stronger tower, new arcades and chancel in the Early English period. Two bays at the west end of the nave, the north aisle windows and the transepts were added in the Decorated phase and the south aisle windows (1464–46) and the porch (1500) to complete the sequence. The fires missed the church and explain the relative paucity of surviving early domestic buildings in comparison with Diss and Wymondham. Emphasis will be placed on the church as a centre for the community in this section.

Nearly all parish churches were endowed with sufficient land to maintain an incumbent. These lands were known as glebeland and most of these allocations are recorded from Domesday Book onwards because of the continuity in church ownership. Care was taken to record them by drawing up regular 'terriers' or lists of those lands. The 1725 glebe terrier gives a full picture of the properties of

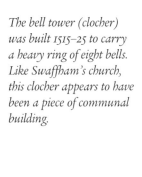

The bell tower (clocher) was built 1515–25 to carry a heavy ring of eight bells. Like Swaffham's church, this clocher appears to have been a piece of communal building.

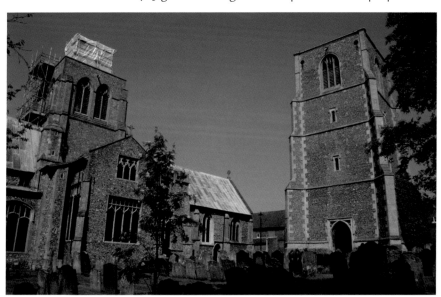

Dereham Vicarage in the early 18th century. This terrier was made at the time of the visitation of the new bishop of Norwich, John Leng. It starts by describing the vicarage as

> a handsome and convenient dwelling house with a parlour, hall, kitchen and other convenient rooms and at a small distance from the said dwelling house there is a convenient study and brewing house all in a garden containing about one acre of land enclosed with a large and clean moat. In the yards without the moat there is a stable and hay house in unexceptionable repair standing in a yard containing by estimation about one acre of land bounden on the east and west by two moats.

Tithe, one tenth of the annual return of crop or stock, had to be paid by everyone and the Dereham terrier gave very detailed rules for the payment of the vicarial tithe, for example, the tithe of wool and lambs at the time of clipping and 6d for every beast fatted in town. The windmill had to pay 8s a year to the vicar and tithe had to be paid on hemp when it was gathered up. Lastly, every inhabitant in the 'body or chain of the township' had to pay tithe in kind for their orchards and gardens! One wonders if the vicar had time to collect all this!

The total of glebe recorded was 22 pieces, amounting to 60 acres. The town, as opposed to the vicar, also had property in the market place in 1725 which included the Cross with the shops, warehouses, granaries, chambers and garrets situated in the market place and let out for a yearly rent of £6. There were also 18 acres of arable land belonging to the town, yielding £10 a year, collected by the headboroughs in order to repair the bridges belonging to the parish and to cover other expenses.

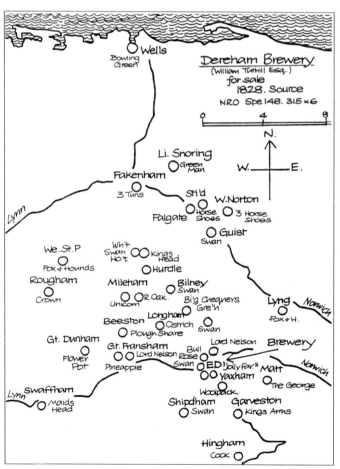

Dereham as an industrial town

A variety of industries developed to serve the agricultural region of which Dereham was the centre. Maltings supplied local brewers such as Tuthills who were already important before the arrival of the railway and supplied a wide area round Dereham with their beer before their sale in 1828. Their brewery occupied a large area bounded by Baxter Row, Norwich Road and Back Lane at the time of its sale. Unlike Diss, Dereham, at least by the early 19th century, had no remains of a textile industry. White's Directory of 1845 shows Dereham having a wide range of services. Six brewers and maltsters must have been major employers but even before the arrival of the railways there were iron foundries, curriers, several schools of various sorts, but no grammar school, cabinet makers and gunsmiths. All these were a step above the range of most market towns but there were also the usual bakers, boot and shoe makers and grocers. The 33 inns, taverns and beer houses underline the centrality of Dereham and the size of the parish is emphasised by the 32 farmers within it. No big estates dominated the area compared with that around Aylsham, for example.

The arrival of the Norfolk Railway from Wymondham to Wells, 1847–49, and the branch to Swaffham (Lynn and Dereham) in 1852 (both becoming part of the Great Eastern Railway in 1862) had a noticeable influence with big new maltings being built along the line.[66] *(See the map on page 73.)* However, compared with the direct route of the Norwich to King's Lynn turnpike, 1770, the railways did not offer a direct east-west route and they suffered in the Beeching cuts of 1968 and 1970. (The demands of the army in using Swanton Morley airfield have led to a reopening of the stretch from Wymondham to Dereham.)

East Dereham breweries and public houses: map by Ruth Murray based on the author's research.

Agricultural engineering was another new industry and in 1908 Kelly's Directory listed steam engines, threshing machines, an iron foundry, a coachworks, sawmills and tanning as well as malting as industries of a thriving market town. The arrival of the railway led to a concentration of maltings on the edge of this industrial area.

As the town grew so water supply, street cleaning, fire regulations, dealing with vagrants and maintaining roads all became increasingly costly. Rates had to be charged for these services and the Tudor governments had enforced a Poor Rate to be charged as well. It was to deal with these issues that a 'council' of Headboroughs was elected to make such decisions.

Dereham as a community

Dealing with the poor was a problem for all settlements after the dissolution of the monasteries when the feeding and care of the poor ceased to be carried out by the church. The Tudor Poor Law, established by 1600, allowed parishes to levy a poor rate following the Act of 1597 which allowed them to set up their own poorhouses (variously called townhouses, workhouses or houses of industry). These were additional to the many almshouses and charities founded by private individuals. Overseers of the Poor were established by all parishes to collect and distribute this poor rate. In Dereham a house of industry was set up near The Dale, on Sandy Lane, but this was demolished in 1775 when the new Union for Mitford and Launditch hundred was established and a large house of industry was built at Gressenhall with its own farmland around it (now the Gressenhall Farm and Workhouse museum and base for the Historic Environment Unit). Dereham then opted out of this arrangement in 1801 and built a new workhouse on the Norwich Road which is shown on Bryant's map of Norfolk of 1826. In 1836, when the new Poor Law was set up, this arrangement ceased and the Dereham poor had to go to an enlarged Gressenhall.[67]

Like the other Norfolk market towns discussed, Dereham was not a borough as Castle Rising, Thetford and Lynn were. The authority of Ely remained supreme in the manorial courts. Ely, with its tradition of Benedictine and then of diocesan organisation, kept control of the working of the town until 1540 and thereafter the Queen's administrators did the same thing. Ben Norton illustrated how the manor court controlled the market in 1635.[68]

> In 1632 Francis Dey and others, common brewers, were presented for selling ale by unlawful measure and breaking the assize, each fined 3d.

> In 1635 a number of millers were presented for the selling of flour in the market by unlawful measure within the precincts of the leete, each fined 3s 4d. Ed Pattrick was presented for selling butter in the market by unlawful pints. Thomas Vincent was presented for allowing his cattle on Northwoode greene next to the way called Dereham Gate.

This last example shows how the grazing of stock was a continuous problem.

After the Dissolution, when Tudor central government was asking more of communities with regard to looking after the poor, criminals, roads, bridges and defence, a body of local inhabitants evolved with powers of taxation. This body was known as the Headboroughs. The provision of good schools is a measure of the importance of a market town. It was not until 1912 that a girls' high school was formed after careful thought as to whether to establish it in Swaffham as a sister school to Hamond's School.[69] In 1915 the Crown School was established. In 1944 this became the Secondary Modern school which is now Northgate High School, providing education up to the age of sixteen for boys and girls, and Dereham Sixth Form Centre. Dereham's population has more than doubled since 1951 and the as yet only partially dualled A47 has at least bypassed the town with one of its all too few stretches of dual carriageway. Dereham is the fastest growing of the towns in this book.

The town sign alludes to the legend of St Withburga feeding the builders of her new convent with milk from two wild does. The local overseer is said to have hunted these does down with dogs to prevent them from coming to be milked.

Fakenham chronology

1700–700 BC	A cluster of Bronze Age barrows near Pensthorpe
500 BC – AD	Iron Age finds at Warham and South Creake and Warham hill fort
AD 60–300	Toftrees, the nearest Roman settlement and road
c. 600	Early Saxon cemetery at Pensthorpe
1066	King Harold held the manor (still a royal manor in 1066)
1200	The Priory of St Stephen (Augustinian) founded at Hempton
1286	Market charters: two fairs on Hempton Heath, that on 22nd November being for cattle
1291	The Priory held lands in 40 parishes
1338	Advowson of the church to King's Hall, Cambridge (Trinity College)
1369	Edward III gave Fakenham to John of Gaunt, Duke of Lancaster
1497	The church porch added
1535	Hempton Priory dissolved (sold in 1546 to Sir William Fermor and his wife)
1602	The church porch used as a powder magazine for Gallow hundred
1631	The manor sold to Knightly, Gawdye and Stubbe
1649	The Sessions House in ruins, Walsingham being used
1650	Thirty and a half stalls on the market in use
1659	A fire in Fakenham and a list of manor tenants produced
1738	A second fire
1781	The windmill built
1794	Ann Harrison's charity for schoolmaster and schoolmistress
1795	The Fakenham Providence Society formed
1801	Population 1,236. Subscription library established
1808	Baptist Chapel built
1819	Independent chapel
1823–28	Turnpikes to Norwich, Lynn and Wells established
1825	Primitive Methodist Chapel built; Goggs' mill demolished
1841	Population 2,158
1844	Norwich Road School opened
1855	Corn Hall built
1857	Railways to Wymondham and Wells completed
	Cattle Market opened
1879	Midland & Great Northern Railway to Lynn and Yarmouth opened
1894	Fakenham did not become an urban district
1901	Population 2,907
1951	Population 2,933
1959 & 1964	Railways closed
1986	Fakenham bypass completed
2001	Population 7,357

Fakenham

The town plan of Fakenham is a simple one, not unlike that of Downham Market, a T junction consisting of the original Norwich to King's Lynn road at the head of the T with the long leg being Bridge Street which runs down to the River Wensum and the mill. The market place and the square lie on the west arm of the T. In that Tunn Street and Mill Lane run past the Manor House down to the mill it may be that this was the earlier route to the river. The Market Place is defined to the west by the former Corn Hall and to the east by the Town Hall, the former Red Lion Hotel. Flint is the main building material of the earlier buildings with brick replacing it later. As the attractive 18th century map of the town shows, Oak Street was lined with properties, as was White Horse Street. The town, like the others being discussed, was compact and focussed on its market place and great church.

North of the Market Place is the striking church of St Peter and St Paul. It dominates the town but as in the other towns it lies behind the buildings which line the

George Stewardson's lithograph of Fakenham market place, dated 1880.

The north side of Fakenham market place.

north side of the market. The church is not mentioned in Domesday Book and the Early English doorway is its earliest feature. In the 14th century rebuilding resulted in a new chancel with a beautiful Decorated east window, chancel arch and lovely sedilia and piscina. Pevsner and Wilson suggest that the main arcades are still 14th century but a little later. The 15th century tower dominates the town; was this the replacement of an earlier tower? Cotton and Cattermole note a bequest by Agnes Heyward to the new tower of 26s 8d in 1447, and in 1492 Robert Bateman left 20s for making three bells.[70] It was being built in the same period when so much church rebuilding was going on in Norwich. Barley and sheep were the most likely providers of this prosperity. Blomefield dates the church porch to 1497 and gives William Rawlyns as having given 20s to the church and 20s to work on the tower.[71] In 1338 the advowson went to King's Hall, a component of the future Trinity College, and one wonders if there was any contribution from the College. In 1369 as

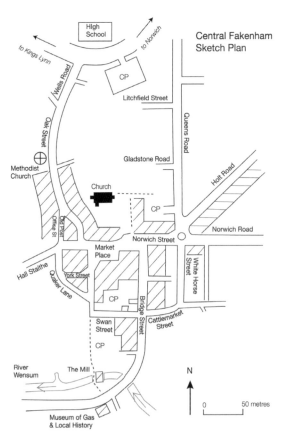

Central Fakenham
Sketch Plan

John of Gaunt was given Fakenham by Edward III again it may be that a gift was made. The major monuments relate to the Calthorpe family of East Barsham between 1650 and 1750. There are no monumental clues as to early benefactors to the church.

14th-century sedilia and piscina in Fakenham church.

Fakenham, as the map shows, lies on the north bank of the River Wensum at the northernmost point of a great loop which the river makes from the Raynhams to the Ryburghs. The headstream of the River Stiffkey lies near Thorpland Lodge Farm just to the north of Fakenham and the stream flows northwards to the sea to the east of Stiffkey. A direct route north from Fakenham

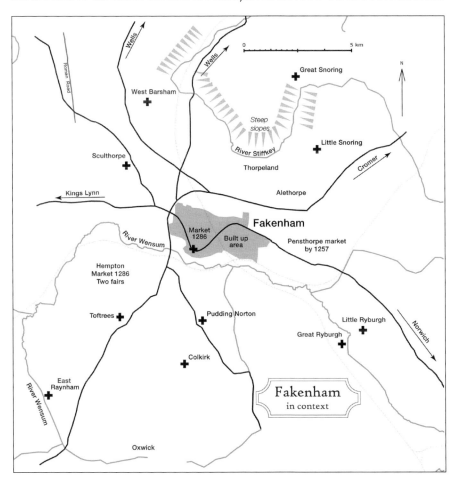

Fakenham in context

runs ten miles to the port of Wells. A Roman road crossed the Wensum two miles west of Fakenham and 23 miles to its north-west lies King's Lynn. Three great estates, Raynham, Houghton and Holkham, lie to the south, west and north of it respectively. This is the zone of 'good soils' and the chalk is much nearer the surface than to the east where the boulder clays thicken. The open chalk plateau provided lands for airfields at West Raynham, Sculthorpe and Little Snoring.

There is little recorded evidence of human activity in the Fakenham area until the late Neolithic and early Bronze Age periods which were marked by a series of tumuli just to the north of Pensthorpe. A scatter of late Bronze Age and Iron Age finds stretches northwards to the coast and Warham Camp is the outstanding Iron Age feature in the area some eight miles to the north of Fakenham. The influence of Rome shows up with finds along the sides of the Wensum Valley and an important road which broke away from the Peddars Way north of Threxton linked Toftrees to the Burnhams on the coast.

A Saxon cemetery at Pensthorpe and two more at Dunton emphasise that there were Saxon settlers in the area. The famous Saxon cemetery at Spong Hill in North Elmham with its vast number of burials raises the question of just how big the Saxon population was in this area. The -ham and -ton placename endings, together with the -burgh element at Ryburgh, all argue for the Saxon naming, or renaming, of settlements. The place names Colkirk (*kirk* = church) and Oxwick (*wick* = an outlying farm, here a cattle farm) argue for some Scandinavian influence, perhaps on to the boulder clay plateau that had not appealed to earlier Saxon settlers.

Fakenham and several subsidiary vills were held by King William in 1086. Fakenham in 1086 was much smaller than Aylsham, for example, though it did have three water mills and half a salt house which must have been on royal land further to the west or north and near the sea. These outliers were really farms, Alethorpe and Thorpland, each of one carucate (120 acres) in demesne. Creake (which one is not clear) was nearly as large as Fakenham in land area and number of villagers.

All the settlements shown on this map were at least in part outliers to the 11th-century royal manor of Fakenham.

In Stibbard the king had three freemen and in Barsham one only. These settlements were mainly small but Fakenham was the focal point for a considerable area.

Of the twelve towns being studied, Fakenham was the only one with a priory on its doorstep. This was an Augustinian house of St Stephen which was founded with only four canons by Roger de St Martin and Richard Ward. Hempton was a tiny settlement in 1086

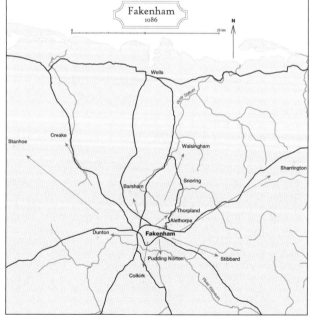

and in William de Warenne's empire. It was in effect a small farm. By endowing it with a market William may have assumed this would give the priory some income. However, Blomefield noted that the market was a considerable one, especially for cattle. It is difficult to see that it could have competed easily with the bigger market in Fakenham but Pevsner and Wilson suggest that it may have limited the growth of Fakenham.

The priory had its own mill known as Brygge Mylle and in 1291 it had land in 40 parishes, often only in small pieces, and a total income of £29 2s 0d. In 1302 it received a licence allowing it to bring back a watercourse through its precinct. An inventory taken at the Dissolution in 1536 gave a valuation of £128 3s 9d. The farm had 20 pigs, five cattle, 125 sheep, 40 lambs and 13 horses and mares for the plough. There was corn standing on 68 acres, worth £13 12s, and barley, peas and oats on 97 acres worth £24 11s 9d. There were only two canons, 15 servants, ten hinds (married female servants) and five waiting servants. Detailed accounts were also given of the furnished domestic rooms of the priory. Although it was small it must have been a significant addition to the life of its neighbouring market town, providing a variety of work.[72]

In 1659 a full field book of Fakenham and Thorpland Hall was drawn up.[73] This book (survey) split Fakenham parish into 31 furlongs. In this context furlong seems to mean a convenient subdivision of the manor, unless it is continuing an earlier arrangement. No field names are given, such as East Field. The 4th furlong included 'the butchers' stalls and such houses as are in or near to the market place with passages round about them'. These are as follows:

ABOVE: *A butcher's stall in the market place in 2011.*

BELOW: *Passage leading from the church into the market place.*

The lord	one stall
Francis Page	one shop
Henry Lawes	one shop
Alice Roberts, widow	nine stalls
—— Lawes, widow	two stalls
—— Alderson	three stalls
Peter Stringer	one stall
William Harridaner	four stalls and a half
Nicholas Fenn	three stalls
Nicholas High	one stall
John Bullayn	one stall
Francis Whitle	one stall

This list was followed by 14 tenements i.e. built-up sites of which three were the almshouses. In the sixth furlong Rice Gwynn Esq had the water mill. In the third furlong there were 11 tenements, one being called The Sun and another The Falcon. Putting the 3rd and 4th furlongs together begins to give us a picture of the core of Fakenham in 1659. In that no mention is made of the fire in the survey it would seem that it broke out later in the year. The large 15th furlong contained 28 pieces of land of which Rice Gwynn held four (of 74 acres) and in which there were 10 tenements, five pieces of glebe and 11 'incloses'. So from this useful survey we can begin to get a picture of Fakenham with its shops and stalls round the market place and the properties to its east and those along the Norwich road. The subdivisions of furlong 15 and of many others as well give a picture of the late medieval layout of the field system of the parish.

*Motor vehicles come to
Fakenham market place,
1913.*

There is no description of what was burnt in the fire of 1659 to compare with that which exists for Wymondham in 1615 or for Holt in 1708, but various accounts have survived that show what a long business it was to distribute monies collected for those most in need. In October 1660 Syderstone, near Docking, collected £1 10s 6d and Soham (Cambs?) collected £1 4s 4d. In 1669 a dividend was paid by Francis Thurston Esq to Sir Christopher Calthorpe for sufferers of the fire to the amount of £33 13s 7d.[74] In 1670 £1 14s 7d was allotted towards Thomas Curzon, deceased, paid to Robert Bloom as a creditor.[75] In 1671 a suit was made by the townsmen against the sons of Taylor relating to the fire and £55 9s, part of £62 13s, was paid by Richard Jessopp, gent., to Sir Christopher Calthorpe 'to the use of the suffering by fire in the town of Fakenham'. No one received more than £2 10s and many only very small amounts. As this was 12 years after the fire these may have been allotments of later collections of money received. So far it has not been possible to make any estimation of the total cost of the fire or of the number of properties burnt.

The period of the Civil War produced a great deal of documentation recording the rates raised to support the parliamentary army. In 1646 Fakenham raised £31 3s 4d and this rate was levied by Rice Gwynne, Robert Sheringham, William Sheldrake, Henry Cock and Richard Bird. The major contributors were Rice Gwynn, £4 13s 9d; Richard Cushing Senior £3 15s 9d and James Palgrave £3 10s 8d. A rate levied in 1649 noted how much land each payer owned. For example Rice Gwynn, a major figure in this period, had a messuage, 12 acres of meadow and carr (marsh), 100 acres near his house and 72 acres remote. William Harridane, gent., owned several tenements, one messuage with 21 acres, 89 acres and 12 acres of meadow. A rate of 16th November 1650 was charged at 6d on every piece of land rated at £1.[76]

*Fakenham: a rate made this 16th day of November 1650
for 6d in the £ for lands[77]*

A sample of the main landowners recorded in this rate is given:

James Calthorpe Esq	123 acres with a messuage in Thorpland	£1 4s 8d
More the said Mr Calthorpe	for 44 acres of sheep's pasture	3s 8d
Robert Lemon and Richard Walker farmers to the said Mr Calthorpe	for 2 messuages 487 acre	£5 0s 0d
Rise Gwynne Esq	a messuage and 259 acres	£3 11s 3d
Richard Wells, cleric	64 acres of glebe and tenths p.a.	£2 12s 6d
William Harridance	a messuage and 143 acres	£1 19s 0d
John Breviter	a messuage, malthouse and 24 acres	12s 0d
William Sheldrake	messuage, malt house and 21 acres	10s 0d
Thomas Spooner farmer to Mr Gwynne	for a watermill	16s 0d

There were 32 tenements listed, 17 messuages, one house, one cottage, three malt-houses, four shops and three inns. James Calthorpe and Rice Gwynne were the largest landowners and several of their tenants important farmers. This rate does not locate properties but many of the tenements, messuages and the shops and inns were clearly the core of the town at that date.

In 1649 there was a debate as to how to repair the Sessions House in Fakenham.[78] The Lord of the Manor, Sir Christopher Calthorpe, pointed out that the Sessions House was begun by one Stibbard as a successful inn and that earlier sessions were held at Walsingham and Holt. However in 1634 Fakenham was certainly one of the meeting places for Michaelmas and Christmas sessions. Calthorpe argued that those who did best out of sessions were innkeepers. In 1672 a letter was signed at the general sessions held at Little Walsingham noting:

> whereas the howse in Fakenham wherein the quarter sessions of the peace used to be kept was at the last general session there holden very ruinous and in decay and also very inconveniently made for the keeping of the sessions therein.

The justices, bearing in mind the fire in Fakenham in 1659, said they would help the improvements to the tune of £20: 'which the court doth give as a free benevolence not as anything due from this county or ever to be drawn into example for the future'. Things have not changed over the centuries! However, by 1730 the Sessions House was 'very old and ruinous and very unfit for holding the said sessions and that the same cannot be any ways be made fitt . . . but by pulling down and

Fakenham water mill, on the Domesday mill site.

rebuilding the same'. The well known architect Matthew Brettingham estimated that this would cost £200. Agreement between the inhabitants of Fakenham for building the Sessions House was made on 4th July 1730. They agreed to pay by means of a town rate specifically for that purpose.

In 1768 the Lady of the Manor, Dame Mary l'Estrange, agreed to allow Mr Hall, schoolmaster, to use the upper part of the Sessions House as a schoolroom. He had, however, to leave the ground floor clear for stallholders. Mr Hall was only asked to pay five shillings for this space. In 1801 the school had failed and a careful inventory of all the school materials in the Sessions House was made: they were sold on 9th December 1801 for £60 3s 4d. In 1794 Ann Harrison's Charity left £10 to a mistress to teach eight poor girls and £10 to a master for four poor boys. By 1845 White lists five academies, a National School and a British School in Fakenham.

Roads and railways

Fakenham became the focus for a trio of turnpikes. The Norwich–Fakenham–Lynn route dating from 1823 to 1828 was the most important but the fact that two turnpikes were made from Fakenham to Wells underlines the importance of Wells as an outlet for local barley and for the importing of coal.

The minutes for the Wells–Fakenham turnpike begin on 8th July 1826.[79] Perhaps the presence of the Holkham Estate was an important factor in setting up the Trust. Thomas William Coke of Holkham was present at the first meeting and, not surprisingly, he was elected chairman. On 23rd August 1826 agreement was reached as to where tollhouses were to be built: there were to be two on the Wells–Fakenham road, one in Wells and one in Sculthorpe. Messrs Blaikie (Coke's bailiff), Ackroyd, Sandys and Elgon put up £500 each towards the costs of setting up the turnpike. By December the toll rates were agreed; every score of oxen was to pay 10d and every score of calves, sheep and lambs 5d. This route survived until 1857 when the railway from Wymondham via East Dereham reached Fakenham and went on to Wells, undercutting the turnpike and also being much quicker. This line finally closed in 1964. The Midland and Great Northern Line from Great Yarmouth via King's Lynn to the Midlands lasted from 1881 to 1959. Fakenham benefited from the railways for only just over 100 years and like Swaffham, Reepham and Holt saw the railway era come and go.

Fakenham market place (looking south-east), photographed in 2003.

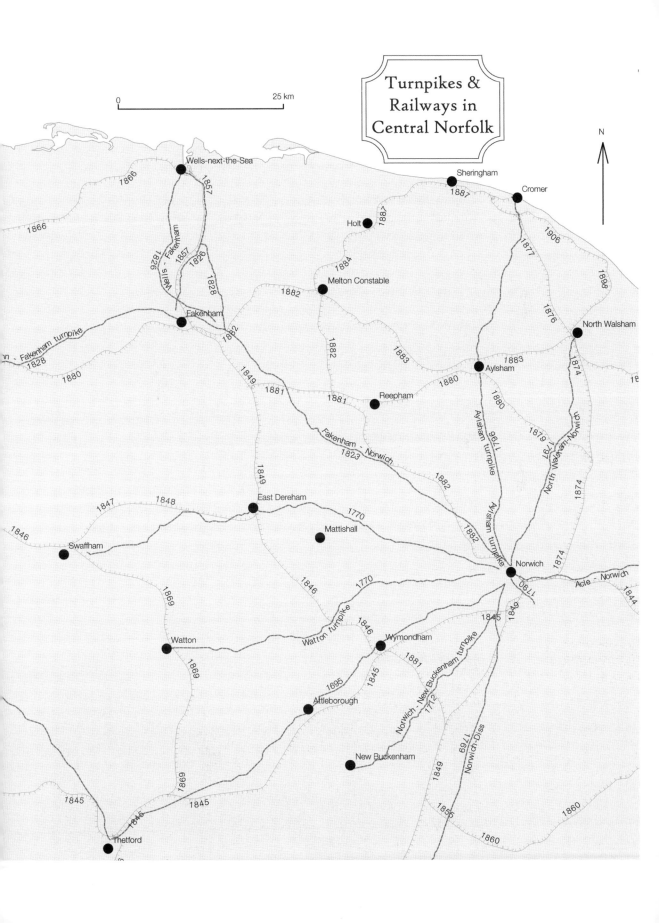

Turnpikes &
Railways in
Central Norfolk

N

0 — 25 km

Wells-next-the-Sea
1866
1857
1866
1866
Wells - Fakenham 1826
1857
1826
1828
Fakenham
1882
n - Fakenham turnpike
1828
1880
1849
1881
1881
1882

Sheringham
1887
Cromer
1887
1906
Holt
1887
1877
1884
1876
1898
Melton Constable
1882
North Walsham
1882
1883
1883
Aylsham
1883
1874
1880
1880
18
Reepham
Aylsham turnpike 1796
1879
1876
North Walsham - Norwich 1797

Fakenham - Norwich
1823
1882
East Dereham
1848
1847
1770
1849
Mattishall
1846
Swaffham
1846
1869
1846
1770
Watton turnpike
Watton
1869
1846

Aylsham turnpike 1882
Norwich
1790
1874
Acle - Norwich
1844
1845
1849

Wymondham
1881
1845
1695
Attleborough
Norwich - New Buckenham turnpike
1772
Norwich-Diss 1769

New Buckenham
1849
1869
1845
1856
1845
1846
1860
1860
Thetford

Harleston chronology

400,000–367,000 BC	Lower Palaeolithic finds around the Hoxne Lake
10,000–5,000 BC	Mesolithic finds in Dean's Pit
1700–500 BC	Bronze Age finds in Dean's Pit
500 BC – AD 60	Iron Age finds in Dean's Pit
AD 60–250	Romano-British village at Needham
500–1000	Saxon place names, collegiate church at Mendham
1086	Mendham Priory, daughter foundation to Castle Acre
1270s	Harleston market and fairs and subdivisions of manors
1567	Thomas Gawdy buys Gawdy Hall and estate
1620	First manor court of Mary Gawdy, widow of Francis
1668	Gawdy estate in the hands of John Wogan
1727	John Wogan dies
1778	John Wogan (2 or 3) dies
c1796	Gervaise Holmes dies
1804	New rectory built, old rectory in Wortwell demolished
1828	Sale of Kerrich's brewery and its associated public houses
1840	Gas works built
1841	Population 1,662
1849	Corn Hall built
1849	W. S. Holmes of Gawdy Hall dies
1855	Waveney Valley railway reaches Harleston
1863	GER reaches Bungay and Beccles
1871	Dukes of Norfolk sell off the Harleston manors and many others
	J. S. Holmes buys Gawdy Hall estate
1896	Wesleyan chapel built
1901	Population of Redenhall with Harleston 2,907
1914–18	Pulham Air Station
1951	Population 2,933
1953	Railway closed to passengers (and to goods in 1966)
1981–87	Harleston bypass
1974	South Norfolk District Council established
2001	Population 4,058

Harleston market place, west side

Harleston

The tithe map of 1839 gives a good picture of Harleston in the early 19th century. As it lies in the Waveney Valley one might expect it to have a west–east axis but as it parallels the river which turns north towards Bungay it is aligned north-north-east–south-south-west. The major route from Diss to Bungay, Beccles, Lowestoft and Yarmouth forms its main spine, the Thoroughfare, and its market lay along a widening of this axis. Its western edge is a remarkably straight line and between that and the eastern edge of the market is a zone of rather higgledy piggledy infill of many tiny little properties which were presumably once market stalls. No doubt, like Attleborough, this long, wide market place teemed with cattle during the auction sales of stock from the marshes. Unlike all the other towns there is no great church forming its focus; this was at Redenhall.

It is the townscape that makes Harleston so attractive. Pevsner and Wilson give a detailed account of many of the buildings.[80] Lying in the south of the county and abutting Suffolk, Harleston still has a number of timber framed buildings; the best known being a 14th century survivor behind Keeley's Yard. The Swan Hotel, a fine surviving inn, has a brick Georgian nine-bay front but in its courtyard the remains of the former timber wall can be seen and a long 17th century wing. Candler's House on Redenhall Road is another fine early Georgian house. Many other buildings along the Thoroughfare and Broad Street and the Market Place show evidence of first floor jetties and interesting pargetting. The northern limit of the town was defined by the station, built in 1855 by the Waveney Valley Railway.

Harleston in its setting.

Setting

Harleston lies on the north side of the Waveney Valley midway between Diss and Bungay. A former Roman road from Kelsale to Needham crossed the valley floor upstream of the present town. The B1116 from Framlingham to Harleston crosses the river just to the south of the town. The main road from Thetford to Yarmouth, the A143, uses the valleyside route on the north side of the river and forms the linear focus for Harleston.

Like so many of East Anglia's eastward facing

river valleys, that of the Waveney was a settlement route for those reaching the area from Europe. It is clear from the evidence of stone axe heads in the South Elmham and Mendham areas that Neolithic people inhabited the area. Air photos show evidence of Bronze Age ring ditches on the gravel river terraces at Mendham, Flixton and Shotford Heath and these were succeeded by Iron Age people in Mendham.[81]

RIGHT: *The Roman settlement at Needham, with its road system.*

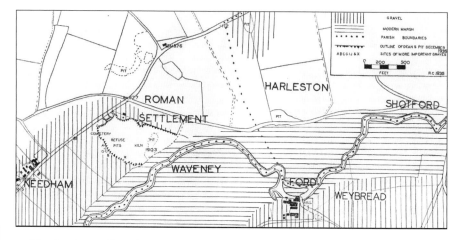

BELOW: *Fragments of decorated Samian ware.*

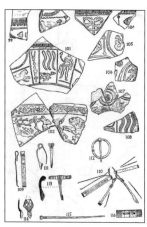

The forebear of Harleston was a Roman settlement at Needham. The evidence for this came from what was known as Dean's gravel pit just to the west of Harleston on the north bank of the river.[82] This pit was cut into a river terrace where Mesolithic flints and Bronze Age pottery had already been found. In 1921, 1937 and 1938 three pottery kilns and a hearth were found. 'A Romano-British village of normal peasant type' was deduced from the evidence of storage/rubbish pits and pottery but no evidence of buildings had survived. It was an early pre-Boudican site that lasted into the early third century. It was a farming community from which querns and mortars survived but late prosperity meant that good quality Samian ware had also reached it. Did it come by river or by the Roman road from Peasenhall via Needham that went on to Caistor St Edmund?

We rely on using placename evidence for the dating of the Saxon settlements; the *-ham* element in Needham and Mendham suggesting primary settlements whereas the *-ton* of Harleston suggests a secondary settlement.

What started as a study of the market town of Harleston has become a more complex and interesting story. This is because there are only two very small references to Harleston in Domesday Book and the land involved amounted to only 25 acres. Yet later references to Redenhall with Harleston and Mendham with Harleston to Needham in Mendham, Shotford in Mendham and Wortwell with Redenhall, all from early days, show that there were complex links between these settlements. Redenhall church lies on the boundary of Redenhall and Harleston. On the Suffolk side of the Waveney lies Mendham. Domesday Book gives a complicated account of Mendham's churches, listing one whole church, a quarter of a church and one eighth of a church. Wortwell, Needham, Withersdale and Metfield receive no mention in Domesday Book. They all lay in the vill of Mendham in 1086.

By 1204 Mendham had a Cluniac priory and by 1270 Harleston had a market. The only nearby markets recorded were those of Diss, 1274–75, Pulham Market

1274–75 and Hoxne in Suffolk where the market was extant in 1086 on the Bishop of East Anglia's manor. As the earls of Norfolk, later to become dukes, were lords of Earsham hundred and held a 'manor' in Harleston their influence was enough to gain a market charter on their holding as it was also to gain in 1259 the right to hold a fair there to last eight days. Blomefield adds to the complexity by pointing out that there were two manors in Shotford 'in Mendham'. These were the manors of Whitendons (Whitehills) and Seameres. Sir Miles Stapleton gave the latter to Mendham Priory when it was joined with Denston's manor in Needham. In 1226 William d'Arches and his wife Eve gave Whitendons manor to the priory of the Holy Trinity in Ipswich. The Freston family were granted it at the Dissolution and still held it when Blomefield was writing. Blomefield noted that 'in the Suffolk part of Mendham there were four manors'.[83] Ryland's map of Suffolk of 1766 shows Redenhall as being in Suffolk! All this shows in what a complex area Harleston evolved.

The earls (later dukes) of Norfolk, despite their varied fortunes in the 16th and 17th centuries, held the manor of Harleston with its market until 1871 when there was a massive sale of their Norfolk property.[84] The manors listed in this sale were Harleston, Forncett, Ditchingham, Earsham, Bungay Burgh, Bungay Priory, Bungay Soke, Fersfield, Kenninghall, Banham Marshalls, Beckhall Grays, Hockham in Banham, Lopham, Bressingham, Boylands in Bressingham and Shelfanger Hall. Lot one was the manor of Harleston, except the market, and lot six was the market of the town of Harleston with tolls, dues, rights, privileges and emoluments thereto belonging. The manor was bought by John Sancroft Holmes and this marked the end of what might be regarded as the feudal phase of this part of Norfolk.

The town that evolved from these complicated origins cuts across the old Redenhall/Mendham parish boundary and in 1885 this part of Mendham was added to Redenhall with Harleston. The tithe map shows it as a linear town with the market at its core. The 19th century parish church is off centre compared with the site of the much earlier chapel.

Priory and church

Mendham Priory lay on an isle in the floor of the Waveney valley. It was founded by William de Huntingfield when he gave the Isle of St Mary of Mendham to Castle Acre Priory for the site of a daughter house. It was built by 1204 when he endowed it with his rights in Mendham church and elsewhere. It was a small house valued in 1291 at only £19 18s 6d. An unnamed author writing in 1900 quoted Spurdens and Gillingwaters' account of 1804. They described the buildings as forming a quadrangle of about 70 feet (33 m) each way. The church lay on the north side of this. The Rant family had kept it neat but when they left it was partly de-molished and turned into a malthouse. It appears to have been 120 feet by 30 feet (56.7 by 14.2 m). A refectory on the east side of the quadrangle was a fuel repository in 1800. The south-west corner of the quadrangle had a timber and plaster corridor with

Part of the tithe map (redrawn from Norfolk Record Office map 222).

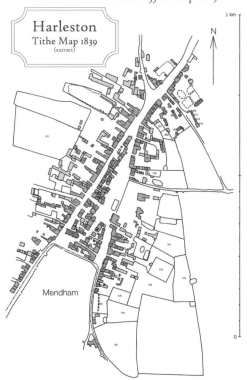

Harleston
Tithe Map 1839
(extract)

Mendham

an ancient oak staircase leading to a spacious dining parlour open to the rafters.[85] It was apparently dismantled in 1815.

Redenhall Church has one of Norfolk's great church towers with high quality flushwork panelling; was this meant to impress churchgoers arriving from Harleston? The discussion by Sandy Heslop of the building of Swaffham church by the 'community' is also relevant to Redenhall. The nave arcades, the chancel and the south doorway show that much of the church as we now see it was built in the period 1280 to 1350,[86] but the full list of bequests given by Cotton and Cattermole in their invaluable article on Norfolk church building shows how many contributors there were to the new building of the tower between 1469 and 1500.[87]

		£	s	d	
1469	William Cowper	0	20	0	
1469	Joan Bunning	3	6	8	
1470	John Mayhell	0	6	8	
1470	Richard Hawk	0	13	4	
1470	Thomas Bacon	0	40	0	
1471	John Poyntras	0	6	8	
1473	William Payn	0	3	4	
1473	John Wytham	3	6	8	
1473	Thomas Tyte	6	13	4	(10 marks)
1476	Katharine Newton	3	6	8	
1484/5	Robert Honeypott	3	6	8	(5 marks)
1487	Agnes Alderych			Bequest	
1487	William Totyll			Bequest	
1492	Thomas Bacon	0	13	4	
1496	Margaret Roche	0	3	4	(Repair of steeple)
1498	Robert Drury	0	6	8	(Tower)

There are similarities with the tower of St Peter Mancroft in Norwich and one wonders if the contributors asked for a tower to be in the style of St Peter; were the same masons employed?

As Harleston grew around its market place so did the need for a chapel. In 1677 Robert Webster of London, a goldsmith, left an annual income of £54 to be paid to Emmanuel College, Cambridge to pay a chaplain and a schoolmaster in Harleston. This bequest implies that a chapel was already functioning.

In 1735-36 leading members of the town launched a fund for the repair of this chapel and subscribers were listed, on a beautifully written list, who contributed £414 7s 6d. The major contributors were John Buxton of Channons Hall with £10 10s, Francis Long of Spixworth with £15 15s and the Bishop of Norwich with £10 10s. Interestingly, Emmanuel, Caius, Trinity, St Johns, Kings, Clare Hall, Queens and Jesus colleges all made a contribution.[88] By 1761 the chapel was too small and a new gallery was added. Finally, in 1872 a new church of St John the Baptist was built on a fresh site and the chapel was demolished to be replaced by the clock tower in the market place.

The first rectory of Redenhall church was in Wortwell and at some distance from it. In 1804 a faculty was passed to demolish this old rectory and build a new one nearer to the church; it read:

> *The parsonage building consisting of dwelling house, barn, stables and neat houses all clay and thatch belonging to the rectory of Redenhall and stands in the most remote inconvenient part thereof and therefore are incapable from their nature and situation of being converted into a residence for the rector.*[89]

The faculty pointed out that glebe land near the church would be much more suitable and requested permission to pull down the old rectory and re-use the materials. It is interesting that the old rectory is described as being of clay and thatch, the traditional building materials of south Norfolk.

Like all Norfolk parishes, Redenhall with Harleston had a considerable Non-conformist population. They too had problems with the provision of a satisfactory place for worship.[90] The first meeting house was built between 1695 and 1698 and the congregation was 'calvinistical in its attitudes'. In 1771 a proposal was made to sell the chapel to Mr Kerrich. A rift occurred in the congregation; some went Unitarian with a preacher and the chapel closed in 1772. James Whitley bought it in that year for the 'Methodistical dissenters' until 1785 when the Calvinists again took control. It was sold in 1785 to James Whiting who gave it to the dissenting congregation in Harleston. He had already built a new meeting house in Wortwell in 1772.

The impressive tower of Redenhall church.

In the 1851 *Census for Religious Worship for Norfolk* Harleston had a Baptist chapel built in about 1820 with only 35 attenders at its evening service. The Methodist chapel in Swan Lane, built in 1827, had an average attendance of 60 and Wortwell's Independent chapel, built in 1772, was well attended with an average afternoon congregation of 146. The Church of England average attendance for afternoon services at Redenhall was recorded as 705 and Harleston chapel of ease 170 for evening services. Given that the census population return for Redenhall parish was 286 and for Wortwell 541, the attendance figures for Redenhall seem remarkably high. Compared with Aylsham and North Walsham the Nonconformist attendances for Harleston seem rather low.

Later changes

The early 19th century saw a number of significant changes in the economy of Harleston. A major change was brought about by the sale of the brewery which by 1828 had become a considerable business, not only in the actual brewery but like Simpson's in Diss, in the ownership of 47 public houses in the area and many other properties in the town and

The Swan Inn: the façade facing the main street (BELOW) is Georgian, but the rear (RIGHT) shows timber framing and a wing with low 17th-century windows on the first floor.

surrounding villages. The brewery was owned by Thomas and Edward Kerrich and a six day sale was held in June and July 1828. The sale notice in the Norfolk Record Office is annotated with the value and names of the purchasers.[91] The manor of Seymours was also included in the sale and a Mr Corbould paid £150 for it.

The brewery was described as capable of doing considerable business and included tun rooms, stores, mill house, mill complete with going gears etc. The plant consisted of two coppers, 20 barrels each, mash tubs, backs, coolers, squares and pumps. Two excellent malt houses containing 70 coom (*sic*) and 20 coom, steeps, suitable for working floors, drying houses and granaries, most substantially built and conveniently arranged. This lot was sold to Mr Norgate for £3,800.

Purchasers and prices were listed against all 47 inns/public houses, The Swan in Redenhall with Harleston, described as an inn and posting house, was sold to Mr Aldous for £1,400. Most of the other public houses went for prices from £450 to £1,000, the median being about £700.

The arrival of the Waveney Valley Railway in 1855 and its completion to Bungay and Beccles gave new contacts with a wider world but like so many of the other towns in this study, its influence only lasted for 98 years and it was closed to passengers in 1953 and goods in 1966. It had two important periods of prosperity, the first when a branch line was built to the Pulham Market airship base in World War 1 and the second when great quantities of building material were needed for the several air fields established in the area in World War 2. Negative effects were felt, however, when two maltings were closed and their production moved to Tivetshall on the surviving railway. Up to 2001 the population had reached 4,058 which was a small increase compared with Dereham and North Walsham.

Harleston's railway station was built in 1855 and closed in 1960.

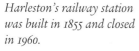

Gawdy Hall

The Gawdy family became influential in the area when Thomas Gawdy (1476–1556/7) became bailiff of Harleston.[92] He had three very successful sons, all of whom were lawyers. His second son, who died in 1588, was knighted in 1578 and was a judge of the court of the Queen's bench from 1570. His influence came from having the Earl of Arundel (a Howard) as his patron. He became MP for Norwich in 1557 and Recorder from 1558 to 1574. He married Audrey Knightly, the daughter of a wealthy Norwich attorney; she died by 1566, and in 1567 he married Frances Riches of Swannington. This progression allowed him to buy Gawdy Hall and lands in Redenhall and Harleston. Sadly the Tudor hall built by the Gawdy family was gothicized in the nineteenth century and was demolished in 1939. He was buried in the family chapel in Redenhall church. Sir Edward Coke, a relative by marriage, described him as 'a most revered judge and sage of the law, of ready and profound judgement, and of venerable gravity, prudence and integrity'.

In 1654 the Gawdy estate, under mortgage, fell to Tobias Frere who bought it. His widow married John Wogan who was lord in 1688. In 1727 John Wogan died and his estate was carefully looked after by his wife Elizabeth and daughter, Sarah. A series of very full domestic and estate accounts survives that throw light on a number of aspects of the estate at that time.[93]

A 17th-century frontage with a 'Dutch gable'.

A valuation of 1779 on the death of a later John Wogan gives a very detailed description of the hall, presumably at the time of its gothicization because several rooms were being built or altered. Outside the main house were a brewhouse, 32 feet by 19 feet, a stable for 15 horses, a coach house for three carriages and a kitchen garden, walled and planted with fruit trees. There were 120 acres in hand and the total rental was £714. The timber had been valued in 1776 but since then a lot had been cut. The whole estate was offered to Governor Dalling for £27,000.[94]

Elizabeth kept her accounts in four parts from 1727 to 1734 with the expenses of John's funeral, domestic expenditure, expenditure on Sarah and expenditure on her son (Master) John. The funeral expenses totalled £259 11s 7d with many individual payments listed but for what was not specified; she gave £5 to the poor of Redenhall. Over £500 went on Sarah's expenses and £872 to John who by 1734 was at Cambridge.

The income from the estate in the same period amounted to £1,355 14s 4d. Several major items were from the sale of beef cattle to 'Smythfield' market. Separate groups of beasts were sold, 21 for £93 14s 9d, 30 for £116 12s 6d, 38 for £142 8s and on 25th January 1727 ten steers for £63. There was £10 15s received for timber and several smaller amounts for the sale of oats. These sales of beef stock underline the value of the grazing marshes to this estate and no doubt to others in this stretch of the Waveney Valley.

Market Place infill between the Swan Inn and Broad Street.

Holt chronology

3000–500 BC	Neolithic and Bronze Age barrows on Salthouse and Kelling heaths
AD 1066	Holt market existed
1086	Holt a royal manor
1253	Cley market existed
1285	Sir John de Vaux, Lord of the Manor
1288	Narford and Ross's manors formed
1556	Gresham's School founded
1588	The Spanish Armada – Weybourne Hope fortified
1592	Outbreak of the plague
1599	Holt Poor House built
1612	Fire in Cley
1708	Severe fire in Holt, the church burnt, only the chancel usable
1754	John Wesley's visit to Holt
1757	Independent church in Holt founded
1779	A workhouse built on the heath
1801	Holt's population 1,004
1807	Parliamentary enclosure, Spout Common allotted to the town
1813	Methodist chapel built
1835	National School built
1837	Wesleyan church built
1841	Gas works erected
1843	New buildings for the National School
1851	Population 1,726
	Erpingham Union workhouse built at West Beckham
	Waterworks established
1884	Midland and Great Northern railway reached Holt
1887	The chancel roof of the church repaired at the expense of Sir Alfred Jodrell
1901	Population 1,844
1907	Further restoration of the church
1951	Population 1,945
1964	The railway closed
1974	Holt within North Norfolk District Council
2001	Population 3,550

Holt

Thomas Kerrich visited Holt in 1821 and, rather surprisingly, noted that 'there is no one thing at Holt worth looking at. Mem. Never to go there again.'[95] Holt lies on the back of the Cromer Ridge which is a great moraine of glacial debris

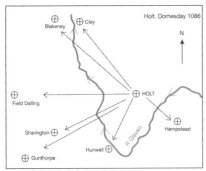

left behind after the retreat of the second ice sheet. This is the highest and hilliest part of Norfolk and the River Glaven, with its odd course, lies in a deep valley. The stream starts to flow south off the ridge but then at Hunworth makes a sharp turn northwards to drain out to the sea at Cley. This area is one of the most attractive parts of the county.

Of all the towns in this study Holt is the only one to have had a market recorded as being in existence by 1086. Cley was the next town in the area to gain a market by 1253. Whether this early market stemmed from Holt's being a royal manor is not certain; it was, however, an important one with berewics (outliers) in several of the neighbouring parishes, as shown on the inset map above.

The Holt area is rich in archaeological finds though little has been found in the town itself. The area of high heath around Salthouse and Kelling to the north of Holt has many late Neolithic and Bronze Age tumuli. Settlement continued into the Iron Age and Roman pottery kilns have also been found. As in so many areas of Norfolk, the early Saxon period has given rise to fewer finds than the mid and late Saxon periods from which a number of metal hoards have been found in the area.

Holt was a large and complex manor in 1086. King William inherited it from Edward the Confessor together with its outstations. The link with Cley is interesting and implies that it was already a valuable port for the manor. The existence of a market by 1086 suggests that it was already an important local centre. Some manors saw changes between 1066

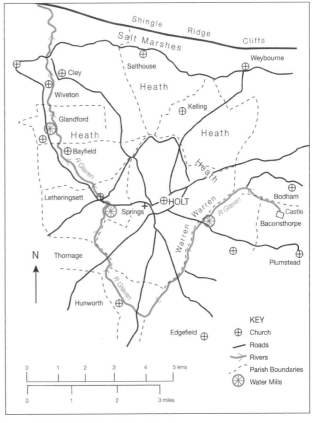

Holt in its setting.

and 1086 but Holt and its berewics changed very little, either in population or in area under cultivation. At both dates it had 24 villagers and 24 smallholders with an unusual entry of 11 men (servants/retainers?) at both dates. Cley and Blakeney, only part of which was held by the king, did not change either during this period.

A most interesting feature of Domesday Holt, apart from the market, was that it had five mills. These were water-powered corn mills using the River Glaven. At this date there was little woodland in the Holt area on the open heaths, only enough for 60 pigs to browse on in 1086. The area was presumably only open heath on the sandy soils of the glacial ridge which would have been grazed by sheep and rabbits. No salt pans were mentioned in Holt's entry. This compares with the Fenland coastal villages and those of the lower Yare valley where there were many. Neither were any fisheries recorded.

By the 1250s Sir John de Vaux held this great manor and many others. In 1288 he died and his daughters, Petronilla and Maud, each inherited half of his Holt holding known (from the names of their husbands) as Nerfords manor and Ross's manor. Two subsidiary manors known as Perer's manor and Hales manor, both including lands in neighbouring villages, were hived off from the main manor. The significance of Perer's manor appears later when it was in Sir John Gresham's hands and providing the initial endowment for Gresham's School. The remnant of the main manor of Holt was finally linked up with Ross's manor by the Hobart and Briggs families in the 17th century. Cley was part of the Narford and Ross manor lands until 1422. If Sir John de Vaux's holding had not been split and interlocked into other complex estates it might have been that Holt would have prospered rather more as North Walsham and Dereham did under the powerful control of the abbeys of St Benet's and Ely. From the 15th century Cley in many ways became more important than Holt because of its trading role.

What then of Holt's ancient market? Lewis Radford noted that Holt market was held in 1190 by Hamon of Hamstead separately from the great manor. This would seem to have been an odd arrangement. Amongst offences noted in the Hundred Rolls was one committed by Thomas of Holt for sending a cargo of wool to Flanders without licence.

The layout of the town

The fire of 1708 was remembered with a number of events in the summer of 2008. Various reports of its impact have been given and a recent discovery at Norfolk Record Office has provided a detailed account of the names of those who suffered and their losses from the fire.[96] It reads 'A true estimate then taken of the loss sustaining in the reall estate of these suffered by the fire that happened in the first day of May 1708 in the town of Holt Market in the county of Norfolk'. The list, in alphabetical order, names 57 owners of property and 16 owners of butchers' stalls. Many owned more than one property; for example, Mr Knowles had a dwelling, two shops, two tenements, a barn, three stables and one mill house for which he was claiming £100 damage. Mr Blyford, the proprietor of 'a house in the market' for annual rent and damage sustained to it and other houses as well, estimated his loss at £520. The Maid's Head owned by Mr Dewing was damaged to the extent of £300. The King's Head, The Mariners, The Lyon and The Cock public houses were also mentioned.

Holt
Tithe Map 1840
(extract)

Houses
Other Buildings
Water

Holt town centre (redrawn from tithe map 494 in the Norfolk Record Office).

The Fishmongers' Company, owners of Gresham's School, estimated damage to a barn and a dwelling house at £140. Mrs Moore, a widow, was recorded as having 'a large new dwelling' damaged to the extent with her own house as well to the tune of £300. The largest single loss was that of the church, estimated at £1,000, and the chancel was listed separately to the extent of £70. A meeting house was damaged to the value of £10. A 'house near the church' belonging to Mr Wilson was also burnt. The estimated total damage listed a month after the fire was £5,387.

The mention of only one house near the church belies the suggestion that the Market Place moved from near to the church to its present site but it confirms the reason for the Georgian appearance of Holt. The rebuilding after the fire meant that brick buildings replaced many that may have been in part timber before it. Some earlier brick buildings do seem to have survived at the west end of the market.

Holt's parish church was much rebuilt in 1727 with a 'feeble' restoration and then in 1862–64 and 1866–74 by Butterfield, who 'over restored it' according to Pevsner and Wilson.

The church of St Andrew lies on the north-east edge of the town. As the tithe map of 1840 shows, the long market place stretches south west from White Lion Street into the High Street which in turn joins the Norwich to Blakeney Road by Spout Common. The south-west limit to the town is set by Thomas Jekyll's striking Methodist church built in 1862–63.

As late as 1840 the town was still just framing the market place apart from a new section to the south of Albert Street which included New Street

ABOVE: *By 1888, Bull Street's market stalls had become small shops, reminiscent of a Yarmouth 'row'.*

TOP RIGHT: *The north end of the market place.*

RIGHT: *Byfords.*

BELOW: *Bluestone Row.*

Plan of the Fishmongers' estate in 1775 (redrawn from NRO Cozens Hardy 11/2/76 Holt box).

RIGHT: *The 1857–60 building of Greshams School.*

HOLT
Market Place

and also a short extension along Norwich Road. Photographs show an interesting mixture mainly of post fire buildings. At the west end of Shirehall Plain is Byfords, a successful delicatessen which has early cellars and brickwork that must have survived the fire. The area of market stalls between Bull Street and the market proper was still in a medieval form in 1840, as was that of North Walsham at that date. In Shirehall Plain the Georgian former court house may have remnants of the earlier Corn Hall within it.

At the east end of the market is the earliest surviving part of Gresham's School which was rebuilt in 1857 to 1860 from the earlier Holt Manor House as shown on a small sketch map of 1775. Next to this to the north is an attractive 17th century group providing an effective end piece to the market place. Some flint buildings, making use of the pebbles from the Cromer Ridge, survive, for example at Bluestone Row, the Victorian terrace on the corner of Albert Street and Cross Street.[97]

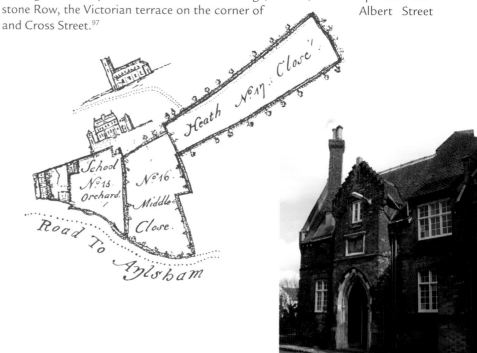

As with Reepham and Aylsham, the arrival of the Midland and Great Northern Railway in 1887 had little impact on the growth and layout of the town and in 1964 under the Beeching cuts it was closed. As so often happens, the former railway provided the route for a new bypass which was built in the 1970s and since this date development has taken place to the south of that road. The impact of tourism on North Norfolk has resulted in the private North Norfolk Railway using the old M and GN track from Holt to Sheringham.

Many will connect Holt with Gresham's School and it must have had and still has a considerable impact on the economy of this small town. In its early phase from 1556 the school was free like those at Aylsham, Swaffham, Hingham and Scarning for boys from the immediate area. Like Jannys at Aylsham and Hamond at Swaffham, it was a local benefactor who made it possible. In 1546 Sir John Gresham bought Perers manor from his brother William for £170. Sir John made his money in London, having been born at the village of Gresham near Holt. He also bought Holt Hales manor and he endowed his proposed school with the income from these two manors and various other pieces of land and three houses in Cripplegate in London. The schoolmaster was to receive £30 per annum.

Hanworth House, on the north side of Bull Street, dated 1744, is a fine example of the three-storey brick town houses being built elsewhere, in Swaffham and Aylsham for example. It may be that the visible flint footings in the gable survived the fire.

A set of typed notes on 'The Free School of Holt' mentions that it had 30 scholars of 'the poorer sort' up to the age of 16 unless they were to go on to the University. Many had done so by 1799 and the school had sent 94 students to Caius College, Cambridge of whom 62 took Holy Orders, seven went into the Law and three into medicine.[98] A further note in the Cozens-Hardy collection recalls that

> the Visitors or any three of them are to examine the highest form and such scholars of that form as they should find fit to go to trade should be obliged to leave the school and such as should be found fit for the University should be recommended thither, and such as profit not should be dismissed from the school.

– a very clear set of instructions! In 1899 the Charity Commissioners issued a new set of ordinances for the school and in 1900 a new headmaster, G. W. S. Howson, pushed forward a major development from that of a small boarding grammar school with 52 boys to a public school by purchasing 56 acres on the Cromer Road for laying out a much larger and more up to date school. Under the new arrangements there was to be provision for 20 Holt Scholars from the town and 20 scholars from Norfolk and by 1908 there were already 200 boys including boarders.

Gresham's School is the name so often associated with Holt but a recent account of Holt Hall has revealed that another very different type of school has occupied the Hall since 1950.[99] The raising of the school leaving age to 15 meant that older pupils in small, isolated schools lacked access to modern secondary education. To combat this Holt Hall became a centre for one-month residential courses for boys and girls up to 16. The then chief education officer, Mr W. O. Bell, and his deputy Lincoln Ralphs, supported the idea strongly. The 78 acre estate provided an excellent area for a wide range of outdoor activities. In 1972 as wider education facilities changed Holt Hall became a residential field study centre, a role it continues to the satisfied experience of the many pupils who visit.

Holt Hall was originally built about 1860 as a private residence.

The building of the new Methodist Church saw the uniting of three earlier Methodist sub groups. A Wesleyan chapel was built in Albert Street in 1813 which was replaced by a larger chapel in New Street in 1838. A Primitive Methodist Society had its own chapel from 1872, now closed; a rift of 1849 had led to a separate Methodist Free Society which in 1863 raised sufficient funds to build the present distinctive United Reform Church. In 1839 land was bought in order to build a meeting house for the Christian Church of Calvinistic Baptists.[100]

The enclosure award

In the eastern part of the parish of Holt there were once large areas of heath and warren, some of it laid out as a race course. Faden's map of 1797 shows roads over the heathland with dotted lines, indicating that they were not fenced off from the surrounding warrens.

The enclosure award for Holt was made in 1810 after the Act of 1807 and it led to a number of changes in the map of the parish.[101] Those that affected the greatest number of inhabitants were concerned with the allotments for those with properties worth less than £10 per annum and also with the water supply.

One hundred and forty properties, listed in the schedule attached to the award, were entitled to use the 120 acres allotment allocated for the poor

that the same shall and may be used by the owners and occupiers of such ancient houses within the said parish of Holt . . . for the purpose of supplying each of them with common of pasture for one head of neat stock or for one gelding or mare and that [they] may, for ever hereafter cut and take flags, ling, bracken or furze for firing . . . to be consumed in such houses and not elsewhere at such times according to the rules laid down by the Rector, churchwardens, overseers of the poor, Visitors and Guardians.

Trustees were to appoint two common reeves and they were to have the power to levy a rate on those who had the rights to use the allotment.

In addition, the Award set out two pieces of land, 'one . . . by measure 13 acres, 3 roods, 37 perches (being the residue of Spouts Common) together with a certain place called The Spouts and one other piece of land of 3 acres 15 perches bounded by Spouts Common, north and east'. These two allotments were made:

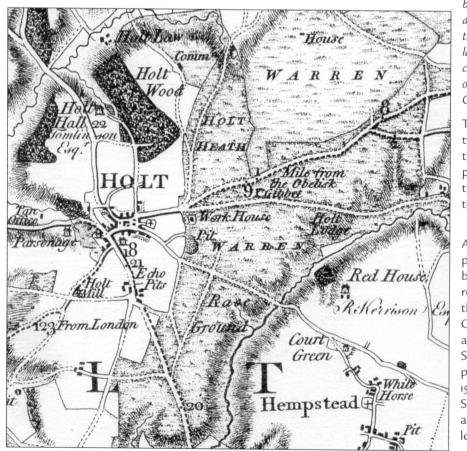

to the intent and purpose that the said place called The Spouts shall for ever . . . be used for the purpose of supplying the inhabitants of Holt with water . . . to be used by the persons now entitled and having rights of common on Spouts Common . . . as a common pasture . . . and not for the purpose of cutting fuel.

Horace Woodward FGS was a distinguished geologist and in 1883 he sent notes on Spout Common water supply to the Erpingham Rural Sanitary Authority with a very nice coloured cross section of his interpretation for the reasons for the strong spring there. He estimated that 10 to 60 feet of sands and gravels lay above 100–120 ft of marls and clay and that it was at the junction of these beds that a strong spring flowed out; it was a question of gradients that brought it out at the Spout. He said the water could be polluted by cess pits but that the filter effects of gravels and sands might explain why there had been no serious epidemics. He suggested that a borehole into the chalk below the clays would give a good water supply.[102]

A further four small allotments were allocated as public watering places for cattle and for their supply of gravels, sand, clay, marl and chalk. These could be used for laying on roads or for providing building materials. Two more 'social' allotments were those for the maintenance of the workhouse built on the edge of the common heath; 40 acres were laid out for the agricultural land to support the workhouse and a further 10 acres to provide fuel, from the heath for the poor there. The Fishmongers' Company, the benefactors of Gresham's School, was allocated a 50 acre plot which included a lime kiln.

The same area, here depicted in Bryant's map of 1826. A great deal of new woodland had been planted since enclosure; much of this has since become Holt Country Park.

The various lords of the manors received large blocks of land in compensation for their various rights which they lost under enclosure. Henry Dampier and Jeremy Smith received a huge block of heath on the east edge of the parish as lords of the largest manor. The Great Wood lay in another block of property to the north of the town which was owned by John Winn Thomlinson of Holt Hall.[103] However, the Great Wood was steadily felled by the owners of Holt Hall.

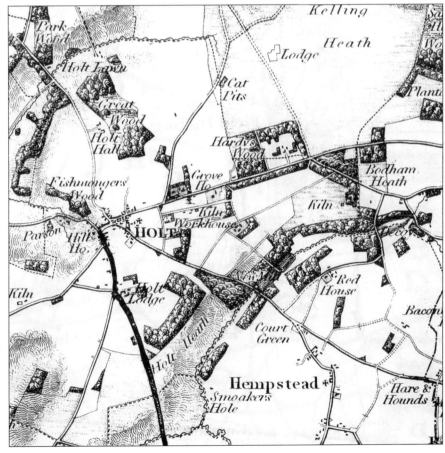

Loddon chronology

10,000 BC	Mesolithic – a few finds in Hales
6,000–1500 BC	Neolithic – a general spread over Loddon and Hales parishes
1500–500 BC	Bronze Age – a concentration 1 km south of Loddon
500 BC – AD	Iron Age – 3 concentrations of pottery 1 km south of Loddon
AD 65–400	Romano-British – large concentrations 1 km to south of Loddon and to the immediate east and west. South to north Roman road along the axis of Loddon
c. 630	St Felix founds Loddon church
400–1150	Saxon/medieval – Hales, Heckingham and Loddon churches, valley side settlement
1086	Loddon church with 60 acres, and water mill
	Lands held by Bury St Edmunds, Robert Gernon
	and Robert, son of Corbutio
1150–1390	Medieval settlement – widespread, major concentration around Hales Green
1209	Loddon advowson to Langley Abbey
1300	Charters for market and fairs in Loddon
1400–1600	Late medieval settlement – less concentrated but still marked around Hales Green
1478	Sir James Hobart buys Hales Hall site and manor
1485	Sir James Hobart builds Hales Hall and Loddon Church and lays out new market?
1492	Guild of Corpus Christi held lands
1503 & 1515	Loddon town lands acquired
1660	The main hall of Hales Hall demolished
1786	A private lunatic asylum in Loddon
1841	Tithe commutation
1857	Loddon school built on Guildhall site
1859	Town fire engine house built
1870	Town Hall built
1894	Wesleyan Chapel built, old chapel 1835
1899	Methodist Hall built – now The Hollies
1901	Population 1,034
1912	The Great Flood
1951	Population 1,082
1951–69	The Tayler and Green estate built
1953	Loddon Secondary Modern School, now Hobart High School
1974	Loddon Rural District Council ended
2001	Population 2,578

Loddon

Loddon and Downham are the only market towns on navigable waterways. Loddon is at the head of navigation of the small River Chet. The Chet has two headstreams that rise on the boulder clay plateau. The longer, called the Welbeck, rises on the northern edge of Brooke Wood and flows through Berghapton and Sisland before joining the smaller tributary that rises to the north east of Hales Hall Wood. The River Chet, as it then becomes, is tidal as far as Loddon Mill and runs for five miles until it joins the Yare at Hardley Cross; it follows a narrow and winding course. Martin George notes that after the 1947 floods it was suggested that the Chet should be closed to navigation.[104] Private boatmen and one still active wherryman successfully opposed this idea. Between 1958 and 1961 four new boatyards at Chedgrave and Loddon were given planning permission. This meant that the river commissioners had to dredge the river and remove obstructions. The river banks were not strong enough to cope with more river traffic; in 1940 the East Norfolk River Catchment Board gave up its attempts to repair the breaks that created the Hardley Flood. Careful measurement between 1965 and 1967 revealed severe bank erosion and by 1976 it was shown that 130 motor vessels a day were

Looking north up Loddon's main street to the River Chet. Holy Trinity church is set back from the market place, overlooking the Chet marshes.

The parish of Loddon.

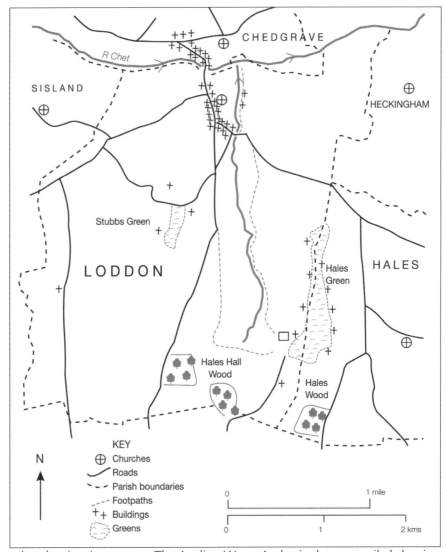

using the river in summer. The Anglian Water Authority has now piled the river over most of its length.

The market town of Loddon lies on a promontory between the River Chet and a small tributary which flows north from Hales Hall to join the Chet downstream of the mill. The area is one in which Alan Davison and a number of colleagues carried out a great deal of intensive field walking which resulted in an important publication on *The Evolution of Settlement in Three Parishes in South-East Norfolk*.[105] This intensive study of the parishes of Hales, Heckingham and Loddon revealed a picture of a long sequence of settlement in the area from the Mesolithic through the Bronze Age to widespread evidence of Roman settlement, less evidence in early and mid Saxon times to late Saxon settlement around Heckingham church and then a marked peak of medieval settlement in the period immediately before the Black Death. This picture of continuous but shifting settlement in the area results from the detailed examination made of it but it may also reflect the accessibility of the river valley and the suitability of the free draining pre-glacial sands of its slopes for settlement and early agriculture; colonisation on to the plateau was more marked in this area than in some other parts of the county.

The Roman period has shown up strongly in the large number of finds in the area with a major concentration one kilometre to the south of Loddon. These finds lie astride a suggested Roman road which ran from Stane Street to Loddon and crossed the Chet at the head of navigation. The alignment of this road is echoed in that of the modern main street.

The west field lay between the town and Sisland parish, Loddon field was sub-divided into Loddon Hall Field and Loddon Town Field on either side of the Loddon to Beccles road. In addition Stubbs Field lay either side of the Loddon to Kirby Cane road and Hales Field at the north end of Hales Green. Fenner argues that

This map of the medieval field system of Loddon is based on a great range of documentary sources.[106]

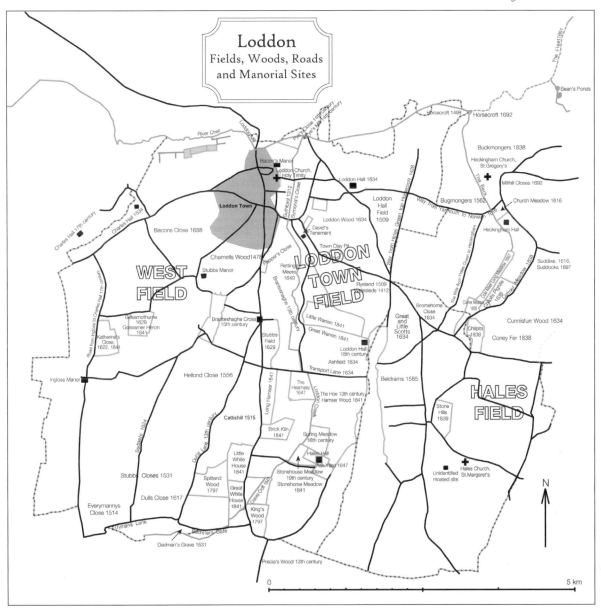

Loddon
Fields, Woods, Roads and Manorial Sites

the evidence was that of a mixed farming pattern. The cropping pattern of lands in Loddon Field, one crop of winter corn and one crop of summer corn and then to summer ley was to be worked according to the 'course of tylth' used in Loddon Field and nowhere else. By the 16th century the earlier strip pattern was giving way to closes in Stubbs Field, for example. The waterside grazings were enclosed early: in the 14th century there was a three acre close of pasture and marsh called Pye's Close next to Pye's Mill.

As there was no enclosure award for Loddon it would seem that enclosure was by agreement. The Loddon glebe terrier of 1709 refers to 'three several pieces lying in the great inclose of Francis Gardiner called Welsteads as the same were lately dooled out with great stakes by the inhabitants . . . with the consent of Charles Humberston, Gent, owner of the inclose'. Woodland remained an important element, both of the economy and of the landscape, in the Loddon area into the modern period.

Hales Green is one of the small number of medieval greens that has survived parliamentary enclosure. As the Dereham references to commons show, the rights as to who should use certain commons and when they could use them formed a source of much debate and often needed clarification. How Hales Green was managed before 1775 is not described but an agreement sealed by all the users of the common was drawn up in order to avoid confusion.[107] In summary, 67 cattle rights were allocated to the owners of the farms surrounding the green of 60 acres. It was to be used only for cattle and no sheep or geese were to graze it. Cattle could be on it from 19th May until the following 1st March but there were to be no stock on it from 1st March until 19th May. This was to let the grazing recover with spring growth. The common fields of Loddon, as with all other medieval communities, would have had complex rules of management as to when ploughing and harvesting should take place.

Hales Green is a rare survival from medieval times.

The town

Loddon consists of a main street running from south to north to the bridge at the mill. The dominant feature of the town is its beautiful Perpendicular church, the origin of which is discussed later. The first church, probably on the same site, must have been much more like those of Hales and Heckingham, perhaps with a round tower and apsidal east end. There was certainly one recorded in 1086 and, by implication, 1066; it was in the vill held by the Abbey of St Edmund of Bury and

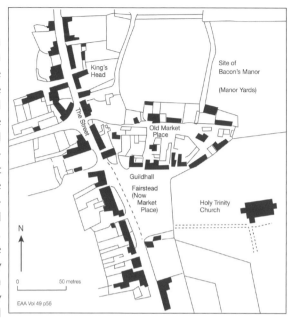

Loddon church and market places.

was well endowed with 60 acres. It was a big vill, 14 furlongs by 9, and there was mention of another chapel in Loddon as well. An earlier market place lay to the north of the present one and was known later as the Fairstead. It is possible that Sir James Hobart may have reorganised the earlier layout of the town in order to set off his new church visually – which it certainly does. The mill, presumably on the present mill site, existed in 1086 but a second small holding in the vill held by Robert son of Corbucio also recorded half a mill.[108]

The street runs from the village cross northwards with a nice mixture of houses ranging from 1600 to 1800. On the south corner of Church Plain is a flint, brick, ashlar building known as the Institute, a building needing further explanation. On the Beccles road are several fine brick houses. Opposite is Farthing Green House which is dated to 1740. Malting House and The Chestnuts continue the gentrified

Loddon House, built in 1711 on the Beccles road, is an impressive five-bay house with three central bays of three storeys and a pediment.

feeling of this area. The team of Tayler and Green were architects to Loddon RDC before 1974 and set a new standard for council houses with Crossway Terrace, Hobart Road and Drury Lane (1951-69). Pevsner and Wilson noted it as a village within a village, setting a new standard for local authority design.[109]

At the north end of the street the mill, a nineteenth century weatherboarded building, is on an old site at the head of navigation. Loddon is developing a riverside sector with new housing, car park and boating facilities. Only Downham Market in this study has such a link because Aylsham and North Walsham both lost their navigations after the 1912 flood.

*Hales Hall had an inner
and outer courtyard with
the hall in the inner moated
court and domestic and
estate buildings in the outer
yard. A series of terraces
and water features lay to
the west of the Hall on the
slope of the small valley.
The nearest Norfolk parallel
in date is Oxburgh Hall,
built by Edmund Bedingfeld
who received a licence to
crenellate in 1482.*

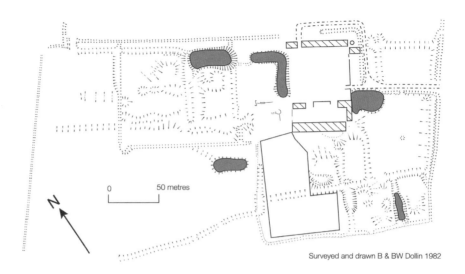

0   50 metres

Surveyed and drawn B & BW Dollin 1982

The Hobarts, Hales Hall and Loddon

The extent to which a family, or families, can influence the development of a town has already been mentioned. In the case of Loddon, it was the Hobarts who had a significant impact. Unlike the story of Swaffham and Redenhall churches, the rebuilt church of Loddon appears to have been solely the work of Sir James Hobart and his wife.

The church of Holy Trinity (1495/6) is surprisingly built of brick but faced with flint which gives the lightness to the exterior. The brick kilns to the south of Hales Hall probably provided the brick for both the Hall and the church. The two outstanding external features of the church are the clerestory and the porch. The clerestory has 15 windows which throw light on to the nave. Pevsner and Wilson regret that the church was 'alas much restored 1870–1900' and comment on the perpendicular aisle windows that they are as 'mechanical as the east window'. Despite these comments the impact of the clerestory and of these large windows is still most effective. The porch, apparently added a little later, is outstanding and it is here that the Hobart shields and initials remind us who built it. The west tower may have been in part the tower of the earlier church but much new work was done on it between 1461 and 1504 when two new bells were added and new work was carried out on the tower and the battlements. In 1504 John Kesses gave 13s 4d and Isobel Hurlebatt 6s 8d for the tower.[110]

Inside the church there are other surprises and reminders of the Hobart dynasty. Sir James and his wife were not buried there but brasses to Henry Hobart (1541) and another Henry Hobart (1561) show them in armour. An impressive tomb chest to James Hobart (1613) and his wife (1609) sits in the chancel. Finally, the last occupant of Hales Hall, Lady Dionys Williamson (1684) is remembered with a striking monument of white marble at the east end of the north aisle. It has been suggested that it may be the work of Grinling Gibbons but it has also been attributed to Joshua Marshall, according to Pevsner and Wilson.

A reminder that churches needed continuous care occurs in a bill that survives for repairs to the church glass in May 1727:[111]

Mr Fuller's bill for glasing att Loddon Church 3 May 1727

For 28 feet new leaded at 3d. per foot	*0-07-00*
For 11 feet new glass at 6d. per foot	*0-05-06*
For 45 querials new glass at 14 for 1s.	*0-03-03*

April 1 1727 at the church

For 359 foot new glass at 6d. per foot	*8-19-06*
For 7 tracell lights and 4 crown panes	*1-01-00*
For worken in 14 cotes of armes	*0-14-00*
For worken in seven cotes with letters	*0-10-06*
For 369 foot new leaded at 3d. per foot	*4-12-03*
For 279 querials new glass at 14 for 1s.	*0-19-11*
Sum is £17.12.11	

Hales Hall lies in Loddon parish and to the south of the town. It was built by Sir James Hobart in the 1480s on the site of an earlier moated manor house. Sir James appears to have had no Norfolk family connections before he bought Hales in 1478. His father, Thomas, extant in 1494, held a manor at Leyham in Suffolk which he left to Sir James' elder brother William. He moved into Norfolk circles when he married Margery Lyhart, niece of Bishop Lyhart. He was executor to the Bishop's will in 1472. It may have been convenient for James to have a base in South Norfolk near to the Duke of Norfolk's estates for which he was steward. These included Bungay, Earsham, the Forncetts and Kenninghall. In his will Sir James left 28 manors in Norfolk and Suffolk that were in his own hands.

Standing high above Loddon with its gatehouse and turrets, the Hall must have been an impressive sight. The surviving servants' wing and the great barn give some idea of the impact that the whole group of buildings, set in a complex of gardens, would have made. Between 1478 and Sir John's death in 1507 Loddon was a Hobart town with its new church and the new market place bearing his stamp.

The great barn and gatehouse at Hales Hall.

The town lands and charities

Loddon, like most of the towns in this study, acquired town lands and by 1492 it had pieces of land in the fields of Heckingham and Loddon. A feoffment (conveyance) of 1509 described ten pieces of town lands totalling 13½ acres all of which lay in Loddon Hall field.[112] The pieces listed are as follows: 4 acres 1 rood, 3 roods, 1 acre 1 rood, 1 rood, 3 roods, 1 acre, 1 acre 2 roods, 1 acre, 2 acres, 1 acre 2 roods. This gives a total of 14 acres 1 rood! Amongst their abuttals were references to the manors of Loddon Hall and Loddon Stubbs. The sizes of the ten pieces show that the medieval field system, with many strips (small pieces of land), was still extant.

In 1566 another feoffment recorded that an agreement was made by which William Gryn, Esq., and Charles Newcomen, gent., received the former lands of the Guild of Corpus Christi and they had granted them to John Blennerhasset and Edward Everard, describing them as 'all that messuage called Davydds in Loddon and Hales with pastures, meadows, closes of the same messuage amounting to 30 acres and consisting of 16 pieces of land lying in the fields of Loddon and Hales'.[113]

In 1595 Henry Hobart, John Humberston, John Clarke, John Cadd, Thomas Belsen, George Bootye, Robert Grimes and William Gales, as trustees, granted to Thomas Langley 'all such buildings or houses with the yards thereto belonging and adjoining called the Guyld Hall of Loddon situate or being in Loddon aforesaid near unto a house there late Henrie Harrison now Thomas Marrett or his assigns . . . paying 5s a year to the above'.[114]

The town lands of Loddon as referred to by White in 1845 would appear by then to have been an amalgam of those in the 1492 agreement and those of the two later agreements to which he gives a total of 80 acres which were being let for £123, the income from which was to be in the main for the support of the church.

In 1680 Thomas Rone, the tenant of the town lands, had run into debt and a detailed inventory of his personal property was made so that it could be sold to pay off this debt to the town. The inventory as a picture of a husbandman's property in 1680 has interesting detail in it. His stock consisted of four horses (one, a black horse, had a star on his forehead), a red cow and three pigs. No sheep were included. His house was quite large: it had a kitchen, parlour, closet, parlour chamber, backhouse and backhouse chamber, kitchen chamber and buttery. In the buttery were 15 pewter dishes, two pewter plates, two beer stools, two iron kettles, two brass skillets, a table, a chopping knife, an iron crane for scales and a frying pan. In the backhouse there was a hand churn, a brewing vessel and a pair of mustard querns among other items. He had wheat, barley and rye unthreshed in the barn and various pieces of equipment including a cart.[115]

The town lands were then let to Thomas Agas on 26th April 1680 when they were described as containing the Town House (was this the former Guildhall?) and 74 acres of land.[116]

Many documents may be needed to make it possible to unravel an apparently simple story. Tracking down the early days of Loddon's Guildhall has proved complicated. Other gleanings come from a variety of sources. In 1831 the churchwardens and overseers for Loddon took out a fire insurance policy. Three units were covered, each for £100. The first, probably Town Farm, was described as a dwelling of stud and thatch; the second was a group of granary barn, stables and outbuildings then or late in the occupation of Philip Beard; a third was for a 'dwelling house now or late in the occupation of Edward Pipe and Widow Fuller part occupied as a charity school stud-built, part tiled, residue thatch'.[117] By 1857 the Loddon School was well under way and the architect was Mr James Benest. A receipt survives for 25th April 1859 for the sum of £12 10s which was a half year's salary for the teacher then in post.[118]

Records of the pre-1859 Loddon School survive from time to time but on 29th July 1824 a visit by Rev. Charles Wodehouse and Rev. Ives Day records the following details.[119] The school had no superintendent; the schoolmistress, Gunton, had a salary of £20 p.a. and there were 120 children of whom 69 were present. Forty-three children had left the year before and 60 new children had come to the school. Children came from surrounding parishes up to three miles away. In the mornings the girls sewed, knitted and plaited straw. It was noted that they attended church pretty well on Sunday. The four teachers were commented on and it was noted that children were often absent at work in the fields. It concluded that 'this school wants superintendence much'.

Various papers relating to the building of the new school in 1856–59 give us a picture of its beginnings.[120] In 1859 a letter from the Trustees to the Charity Commissioners referred to the fact that the school, already built in 1857, had been built on a piece of land containing 16 perches or thereabouts on the site of a messuage called the Guildhall and an adjacent building used as a schoolroom and engine house. These buildings were to be erected in the place of the said messuage and building to be used for a school 'for the education and benefit of the labouring, manufacturing and other poor classes of the said parish of Loddon and as a residence of the master and mistress of the said school'. The letter pointed out that the original contract with William Griffin was for £719 10s but that the final cost was £1,036 14s 8d. This had been paid for by subscriptions of £366, a grant from the Town Estate of £500 leaving an outstanding balance of £171 which was also provided from the Town Estate. A letter from six tradesmen with no date to it, presumably 1857, asked for a delay in starting the building until the spring weather because the brickwork would suffer. They proposed to keep the old building in repair over winter at no charge to allow this. It seems that the provision of facilities for the community were no easier in those days than they are now!

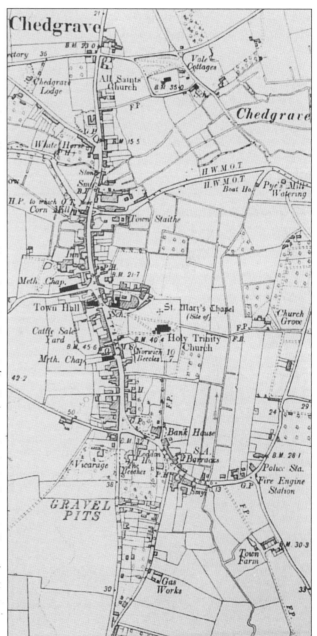

Loddon in the Ordnance Survey map of 1908.

North Walsham chronology

c. 900,000 BC	Happisburgh – the oldest man-made tools in Britain
c. AD 500–800	Saxon colonisation of the area
c. 800	Founding of St Benet at Holme
1020	The refounding of St Benet at Holme by King Canute (1016–35)
1066–86	The vill of North Walsham in the ownership of St Benets
1274	The market founded
1379	Population of 350 taxpayers – weavers mentioned
1381	Peasants Revolt – the Battle of North Walsham
1415	North Walsham selling cloth to Bromholm Priory
1538	The Dissolution of the Monasteries but St Benets transferred to the Bishop of Norwich
1600	The great fire
1604	Statutes for Sir William Paston's school formulated
1608	Sir William Paston's death and monument in the church
1641	Parliamentary Survey of the Manor of North Walsham
1797	Norwich to North Walsham turnpike opened
1808	Parliamentary Enclosure Act and Award in 1814
1825	North Walsham and Dilham Canal opened
1834	The new Poor Law – the poor move to Sheringham and Gimingham workhouses
1851	Population 2,911
1874	The main station opened – Norwich to Cromer
1881	Town station opened – Great Yarmouth to King's Lynn
1884	The poor move to Smallburgh workhouse
1891	Population 3,981
1951	Population 4,733
2001	Population 11,998

North Walsham

The hundred of Tunstead

North Walsham is central to a ring of 12 parishes and this suggests that it occupied an early focal point in the settlement of this part of north-east Norfolk. The small River Ant defines its boundary with the six parishes to its north and east. The upper stretch of Skeyton Beck divides it from Felmingham. The bulk of this part of the county lies in the rich loam zone though the south-western part of the parish is sandier and remained as heath until the early 19th century. The floor of the Ant valley is a zone of marshy grazing land.

Much important work on place names in this area has been carried out by Dr Karl Sandred and it is interesting to see if the names of North Walsham and its neighbours give us any clues as to the sequence of settlement in the area.[121] No major Roman roads are recorded in this area; the important west–east road lay just to its south through the pottery producing area of Brampton and then, most probably, to Caister-by-Yarmouth. No south–north Roman road is known to have run through the 12 parishes.

North Walsham may simply be the home of W(e)alh, a name noted only as early as the 7th century, but it has been suggested that Wal name elements may refer to surviving Celtic people having inhabited the area. Felmingham suggests a place of earlier significance. Honing and Antingham seem to be rather earlier place names, Honing from Haningas 'the people by the Han' (Old English for stone or rock – where or what rock is not explained).[122]

The *-tons*, of which there are six out of the 12 parishes, imply secondary settlements to the earlier *-ham*, *-ingaham* and *-ing* names. The name Swanton Abbot reveals that it was a parish belonging to the Abbey of St Benet. Westwick suggests a dairy settlement to the west of Worstead and the *-stead* element there implies a homestead or farm. Sandred suggests that Witton may be derived from Widu-tun, the *tun* by the wood, and, of course, woodland has survived in the area with a long documentary past. Swafield is interpreted as being simply a field through which there was a track; was this an outlying field to North Walsham that became a satellite settlement? Bacton, Paston and Knapton are all suggested by Sandred as carrying personal names from the originators of those settlements.

The Abbey of St Benet at Holme had a long pre-Conquest history, having been founded *c.* 800, then destroyed by the Danes and revived by King Canute in 1020. This north-eastern corner of the county was well endowed with churches and manors by 1086. Domesday Book carries details of these parishes abutting North Walsham: Antingham, Swanton Abbot, Felmingham, Paston, Witton, Worstead and Honing, all held by St Benet's. These are only a part of the St Benet's possessions which total 65 separate entries, the bulk of which lie in these eastern hundreds. Any great abbey needed a variety of endowments to ensure that its necessary range of supplies could be provided. One manor might provide barley and another cattle or sheep; a major supply of timber was always going to be important to Norfolk monasteries where good building stone was not available. In many cases, for example Wymondham, the market developed near to a monastery; North Walsham, some 11 miles from St Benet's, seems to have fulfilled that

The ancient fields, heaths and commons of North Walsham.

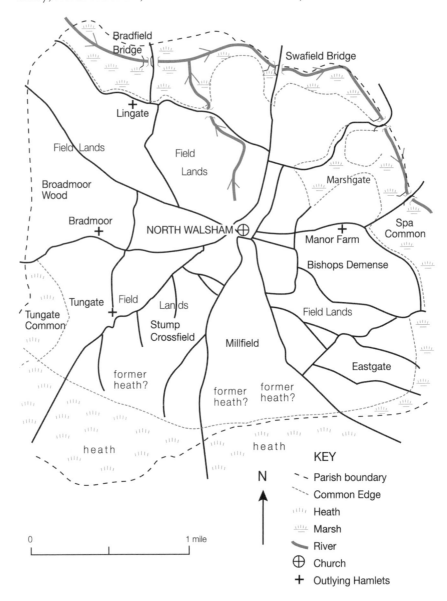

function rather than Ludham which is much nearer to the Abbey. St Benet's held the lordship of Tunstead hundred and this may have been a factor favouring it.

North Walsham did not have a market recorded in 1086 but by 1260 there was one at Tunstead; North Walsham's market is dated by Dymond to 1274/5 and Worstead had one by 1336. The St Benet's holdings vary greatly in size within the various vills, some (such as North Walsham) involve most of the vill and the church, others were perhaps only three freemen (as at Barton Turf) and were only small parts of complex vills divided between several lords.

The register of the Abbey of St Benet of Holme has many references to lands in North Walsham in the 12th century and these are amongst the first details we have for land holdings in the parish.[123] In 1127 Abbot Conrad gave a grant for food and farms to the monks of St Benet's of land which Aylward and his wife Leflada held in Hoveton and North Walsham. In 1141–49 references are made to lands in the field and meadows given as marriage gift. In 1175 a grant was made by the Abbot to Reginald of land in return for 22 pence a year to be paid to the Abbot and of two shillings to be paid to the Hall (*Aula*). There are several other references to the Hall of the Abbey in North Walsham, but none of them tells us where it lay in the parish.

Most informative of all is a grant of 1186–1210 to Elias and John for a tenement held by their father Adam.[124] The lands consisted of 10 acres in the messuage with wood and grazing, nine acres in Millcroft, 23 acres in Eastfield, 12 acres in Southfield, two acres in the brewery (heath), 10 acres in Hagene. There are also references to parts of fiftings which, perhaps, were furlongs. The references to the various fields and parts of 'fiftings' give a total of over 82 acres. This is a yeoman farm in 16th century terms and shows that some farmers had built up their holdings well before the effects of the Black Death (1349). The many references to North Walsham in these two volumes give no mention of a market or to flocks of sheep and only one or two give any clue as to the nature of the 12th century town.

As well as St Benet's, North Walsham was near to Bromholm Priory. The accounts of the cellarer for the Priory for 1415–16 have been transcribed by Lilian Redstone.[125] In these accounts William Paston, perhaps an ancestor of Sir William, was supplying cloth to the Priory. This account shows the local fabric was being bought by the cellarer and reads:

> *Of which he accounts in payments made for 14¼ ells of narrow cloth bought from William Paston draper of North Walsham for the gentleman 28s 6d, price 2s the ell. And in 22 ells of broad-cloth blue, bought for the same, 51s 4d price 2s 4d the ell. And in 6 ells of green cloth bought for William Mundys, 6s price 12d the ell. And in 39¼ ells of narrow cloth for the officers 65s 5d price 20d the ell. And in 33½ ells of broad-cloth of the colour 'soppys in wine' bought for same 55s 10d price 20d the ell. And for 28 ells of narrow cloth bought for the grooms 30s 4d price 13d the ell. And in 22 ells of taw-coloured broad-cloth bought for the same 33s 9d price 18d the ell. And in one fur bought for the Vicar of Dilham 2s 6d.*

This quotation shows how many laymen were members of the Bromholm community.

Stump Cross, now near the water towers on the Norwich Road, is close to the site of the supposed 1381 battle.

ABOVE: *The market cross replaces one erected in 1549 but burnt down in 1600.*

BELOW: *Kett's House, on the corner of the Mundesley and Cromer roads, dates from the early 17th century.*

Peasants' Revolt 1381[126]

Discontent with the social divisions of society followed the impact of the Black Death of 1349. Wat Tyler and Jack Straw led a rebellion in London which was triggered off in opposition to the third poll tax of 1380. A number of riots took place in East Anglia and a particularly well supported one occurred in Norfolk, led by Geoffrey Litster, a weaver from Felmingham (a village two miles to the west of North Walsham) and Sir Roger Bacon of Baconsthorpe. After gathering on Mousehold Heath, as did Kett's men in 1549, Litster's force entered Norwich unopposed but then carried out 'a terror against individuals and buildings associated with the governance of town and country'. The chief opponent of this gathering was the Bishop of Norwich, Henry Despenser. On 25th and 26th June the rebels decided to block Despenser's force just to the south of North Walsham. Differing accounts are of a battle or of Despenser's force causing the rebels to flee without a fight. Having caught Litster he hanged him and quartered his body for display in Felmingham, Norwich, Gt Yarmouth and Lynn. The site of 'the battle' is marked by a cross just to the south of the town.

The Great Fire of 1600

On 27th June 1600 Sir John Popham, Lord Chief Justice, wrote to William Redman, Bishop of Norwich, and Nathaniel Bacon, Sheriff of Norfolk, 'sithence my cominge from Norwich I have thought how the miserable estate of North Walsham might best be relieved' and he proposed the raising of a subscription for poor relief.[127] A short account copied into the churchwardens' records quoted in the Bacon Letters says that the fire began on the evening of 25th:

> in the house of a poore and lewde person one Dowle . . . who flying uppon it is apprehended and in the gaole and by all likelihoode was the author of yt. At least 118 dwellings were destroyed, along with the market cross and all the barns, warehouses and stalls in the market area the loss being estimated at £20,000. The church was also affected . . . in 1601 the wardens paid out £25 15s for repairs to the porch . . . they noted that the country around North Walsham was barren of timber for rebuilding and petitioned the Queen to donate and sell at reasonable sizes from her own woods in the vicinity 'where the tymber is for the most parte small and decaying (and not fit for any use of shipping)'.

The town centre

After the fire North Walsham was rebuilt in brick. There was plenty of good brick earth in the area. Pevsner rather cuttingly says that apart from the church and the market cross 'there is nothing to see at North Walsham of the first order, and little of the second order but much which is pleasant'. The shops around the market place date from the 18th and 19th centuries. Those on the east side against the churchyard are narrow and built on sites of earlier stalls. Perhaps it is the scale of the buildings that gives it a pleasing unity for the busy centre of the town. The market cross dominates the north end of the market and to its east a nice confusion of properties marks the site of the former Shambles. Several large inns form key points and the core buildings of Paston school date from 1765; their great claim to fame is that Horatio Nelson was at school there from 1768 to 1771.

LEFT: *North Walsham market place still serves its original purpose, though the area for temporary stalls has been much reduced by 17th- and 18th-century buildings.*

BELOW: *North Walsham in the 1700s: a reconstruction.*

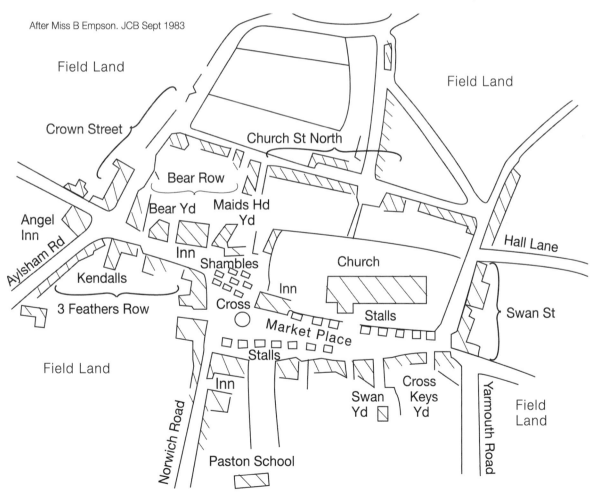

After Miss B Empson. JCB Sept 1983

Field Land

Field Land

Crown Street

Church St North

Bear Row

Angel Inn

Bear Yd

Maids Hd Yd

Aylsham Rd

Inn

Shambles

Kendalls

3 Feathers Row

Cross

Inn

Church

Stalls

Hall Lane

Swan St

Market Place

Field Land

Stalls

Inn

Norwich Road

Swan Yd

Cross Keys Yd

Yarmouth Road

Field Land

Paston School

From court books, inventories and wills we can go a little further in fleshing out a picture of the lives of the farmers and craftsmen of the town and parish in the 17th century. A court book entry for 15th October 1655 includes a surrender (handing over) of the estate of the three Pull sisters, Dorothy, Ann and Margaret.[128] Their property included a lot of the market stalls and shops and the description is as follows:

> At this court comes Dorothy Pull, Ann Pull and Margaret Pull and did surrender into the hands of the Lord of the Manor one butcher's stall situate in the markett of North Walsham late of Margaret Ward and also three stalls lately wasted by fire situated in the markett of North Walsham whereof one stall contained in length XI feet of soil in the markett aforesaid and the other two stalls were lately built by William Haynes in the said markett and containing in length XVII feet and in breadthe XII foot late of John Toppes and Dorothy his wife. And one butcher's stall containing in length IX foot scituate in the markett of North Walsham abutting on the lands late of Edward Dye towards the east late of William Moone and also one stall built in the markett of North Walsham late of Thomas Rolfe.

A rental of the Bishop's manor for 1619 gives 64 tenants.[129] In terms of social divisions those with over 50 acres might be described as yeomen and those with ten or more acres as cottagers, those with less than ten acres as labourers or crafts-

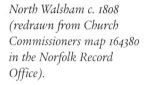

North Walsham c. 1808 (redrawn from Church Commissioners map 164380 in the Norfolk Record Office).

men, e.g. carpenters living by their skills. At this date many craftsmen would also have enough land for a cow or two, hens and pigs and for growing vegetables.

In 1641 Parliament ordered that all royal possessions and church properties be surveyed with a view to establishing 'the real value' of properties as opposed to the rentals being charged on long leases. The North Walsham survey of the Bishop's manor began with a description of the site of the manor:

> The site of the Mannour of North Walsham with a small ffarmhouse, with a barn, stable and other outhouses with a garden and yards thereunto belonging, containing by estimation seven severall enclosures lyeing together next the site of the said Mannour in the north part (est) 27 acres.

> Four severall enclosures lyeing together being divided from the site of the said Mannour by a highway on the south part of the said land – Bures, containing by estimation 24 acres.

> It appeareth that Edmund late Bishop of Norwich thereof of October the 3rd of Elizabeth Regina did demise the said particulars unto the said Queen for the term of eighty years yielding and paying for the same the sum of £2 13s 4d yearly, and Mr Robert King is by assign the immediate tenant.

> The number of acres of the aforesaid particular is by (est) 53.

> The value of the same in 1641 £33 10s.

> An old dove house with the ground and pond thereunto belonging being encompassed with the demesne lands on all parts (est) one acre.

This interesting description of the manor site does not help with the problem of knowing where the manor house actually was in 1641. Further in the survey there is reference to the market and the stalls and shops around it. Twenty stalls are listed and a similar number of shops, some being noted as half shops. For example, Nicholas Poll held several shops and stalls, Widow Goddard four stalls, Edmund Thaxter four shops and Robert Woodyard three stalls and a half. In this same survey the first few entries of copyhold rents show a range of holdings from William Brook Gent with a messuage and 60 acres to James Brante a tenement and eight acres and Philip Beales with a cottage and no acreage given. However, the survey notes that the manor extended into Worstead, Swafield, Bradfield, Felmingham, Antingham and Witton, the total area of copyhold lands being 1,410 acres with an annual value of £710. The names of copyhold tenants are given plus some freeholders so that we have a remarkable list of the tenants of the manor for 1641.

Another way of finding out some idea of the size of a town before the census of 1801 is provided by the hearth tax figures for 1664.[130] North Walsham by that date had 262 houses liable to tax and a further 387 that were exempt. The Scarburgh family had 10 hearths as had the Widow Richardson and Robert Greene. Many listed had only one hearth. Those too poor to pay church rate or poor rate or inhabiting a house worth less than 20s per annum were exempt and had to have a certificate to say so. North Walsham parish had 649 properties whereas Aylsham had 518 of which 385 were exempt. Both parishes are large with outlying hamlets so that the market core of the two towns would be a good deal smaller than these figures.

As with the other market towns in this study there is an excellent account of

RIGHT: *North Walsham
church from the south-east.*

BELOW: *Sir William Paston's
tomb.*

BOTTOM: *The church tower
from the west.*

the parish church of St Nicholas in Pevsner and Wilson. The church is a big one; its outstanding feature is the jagged remnant of its great west tower which fell in 1724 and was never rebuilt. It is a building of the Decorated (1290–1350) and Perpendicular (1350–1530) styles and is a preaching church with no chancel arch. When approached from the market place it is the south porch that strikes one; built *c.* 1380, it carries the arms of Edward III and his son, John of Gaunt. The church's link with the later story of the town is the magnificent tomb of Sir William Paston (1608). This fine monument was commissioned by Sir William two years before he died and has a laudatory epitaph which he wrote himself!

Sir William, one of the last of the famous Paston family, was the founder of that all important element of any market town, its grammar school. The Paston School continues as a sixth form college. The school lies opposite the church behind the line of shops on the south side of the market. The church and school provide the major focal points of this central part of the town.

Social provision in North Walsham

The two previously published studies of North Walsham in the 18th and 19th centuries give full details of North Walsham's problem in dealing with its poor from 1700 onwards.[131] In 1768 the town realised that its earlier workhouse was not large enough and that several small pieces of charity land gave a small return so it was decided to sell them and buy a piece of land on which to erect a new workhouse. The transaction of this change involved copyhold lands and thus a full account, not before published, is to be found in the Manor Court Book for 1767–78.[132]

> *Whereas the very great burthen of the poor of the said parish of North Walsham and the continual increase thereof have occasioned the inhabitants . . . to take into consideration the means of their future better maintenance and employment and whereas at divers meetings of such inhabitants . . . legally summoned and held for that purpose it hath been the unanimous opinion of the persons present at such meetings that a piece of land should be purchased and an house built thereupon for the future habitation*

and employment of the poor desirous of receiving relief in the said parish. And whereas such piece of land hath been purchased and a commodious house for the purpose aforesaid is now building thereon and in great forwardness the expense whereof to the said parish will amount to £1000 or upwards.

It was decided to sell several small pieces of the town lands in order to pay for the cost of the new workhouse. The post-1834 workhouse was built in Smallburgh in the re-organised New Poor Law system of workhouses for each of, or a combination of, the ancient hundreds.

Road, water and rail

In 1797 the Norwich to North Walsham road was made into a turnpike but, surprisingly, unlike Aylsham it was not continued to Cromer, the nearest small port to North Walsham. In 1825 the River Ant was 'canalised' from Dilham to Antingham. Locks had to be made where the canal passed the mills at Briggate, Ebridge, Bacton Wood and Swafield. This did not lead to a separate canal section of the town developing in the way it had at Aylsham. Nevertheless a number of small mills developed as, for example, the bone mills at Antingham.

As elsewhere in Norfolk the arrival of the railways changed earlier patterns of distribution. In 1874 the main station was opened and the line was completed to Cromer High Station by 1877. In 1881 the Town station was opened by the Eastern and Midlands Railway, to be taken over in 1893 by the Midland and Great Northern Joint Railway. In 1897 the Cromer express was providing a non-stop service between Liverpool Street and North Walsham, reaching Cromer in two hours 55 minutes![133]

In 1851, before the railway arrived, North Walsham had a population of 2,911; by the end of the century it was 3,981; by 1951 it was 4,733 and in 2001 it had grown to 11,998. It has, unusually for the smaller market towns, kept its railway line but expresses no longer run non-stop from London. The River Ant, however, a surprisingly small stream, has reverted to being a parish boundary and wherries no longer link North Walsham with Dilham and Yarmouth.

ABOVE: *Decaying lock at Ebridge Mill.*

BELOW: *A bridge on the Dilham and North Walsham canal.*

The twentieth century

The survival of the railway and the arrival of the car have meant that North Walsham has continued to develop. A large area of housing has developed to the east in what is called the 'new town' between Spa Common and the Happisburgh Road. As so often happens, the use made of the old M and GN railway line as a bypass led to the inevitable infilling to the north of the town as far as what is now the B1145 with a growth of light industry beyond. The area of the old town is a very small proportion of the town today.

The early link of the Domesday settlement to the powerful Benedictine Abbey of St Benet at Holme has gone. The ruins of St Benet's isolated on the north bank of the Bure still have great atmosphere that has lasted despite the Dissolution. A timespan lasting as long as the Abbots of St Benet's through to the Bishops of Norwich, who remained as Lords of the Manor and holders of the advowson, has provided us with a magnificent archive.

Reepham chronology

1500–500 BC	Bronze Age metalwork at Hackford Hall
AD 43–400	Roman Road from Billingford to Brampton through Whitwell Hall grounds
400–1050	Saxon place names *-ham* and *-ton*; names denoting woodland – Foxley, Wood Dalling and Salle
850–950	Danish place names, e.g. Themelthorpe and Guestwick
1086	Names of the four parishes of Hackford, Kerdeston, Whitwell and Reepham all in Domesday Book
	Hackford and Kerdeston churches recorded
	William de Warenne held Kerdeston and Hackford and Ralf de Bellefago held Whitwell
1211	References to Whitwell Mill and Hackford Mill
1256	Whitwell church presented to Pentney Priory. Whitwell a vicarage
1275	William de Burgulion held a manor in Reepham
1279	Grant of a weekly market in Hackford
1378	William Gambon held Whitwell manors
1540	Burgulions in the hands of the Sheltons, later the Pastons
1542	Hackford church and rectory burnt, consolidated with Whitwell church
	Rosses manor sold to Ralph Symonds thereafter Whitwell Symonds
1582	Eynsford hundred sold by Lord Morley to Sir Thomas Hunt
c. 1680	Messenger gave both Whitwell manors to Monsey
1743	Bronze Age hoard found at Hackford
1801	Population total for the four parishes 1,726
1806	Buxton House of Industry opened
1808	Enclosure award for Hackford and Whitwell
1840	Tithe awards for all four parishes
1849	Aylsham Union Workhouse opened (St Michael's Hospital)
1851	Total population 1,800
1881	East Norfolk Railway opened as far as Reepham
1882	Lynn to Fakenham railway opened
	Bircham's brewery sold
1891	Leamon's tannery fire at Whitwell
1901	Total population 1,422
1951	Population 1,413
2001	Population 2,455

Reepham

(The Parishes of Reepham, Kerdiston, Whitwell and Hackford)

The 'town' of Reepham is mainly in the former Hackford parish; a tongue of Whitwell parish reaches into it to include the church and the eastern edge lies in Reepham parish. To complicate matters further, Reepham parish church is also the church for Kerdiston parish. There was formerly a chapel in Kerdiston standing in a close on a hill called the Chapel Close.[134] Whether this chapel was a descendant of an original parish church is not clear.

The area covered by the four medieval parishes lies on the boulder clay plateau between the Bure and Wensum valleys. Two small valley systems drain southwards to the Wensum at Lenwade, the streams of which meet at Whitwell Common. The modern town of Reepham, known as Hackford Market in Parson Woodforde's day, lies on a promontory between these two small valleys. The Eyn is the name given to the eastern stream which rises in Wood Dalling parish. The hundred name of Eynsford is assumed to be derived from a ford point across the Eyn. This is a small stream and ford points could never have been difficult to deal with so the exact location is not clear. However, Cameron and Gelling both suggest it is derived from a personal name Aegen as in Aynsford in Kent.[135] A pattern of woods, commons and open fields lay around these four settlements. The wet boulder clay plateau contained several woods, of which the nearby Foxley Wood is the only survivor; farm names such as Primrose Farm, Wood Farm, Oak Farm and Haw Wood suggest that there was once more woodland. The valley floors (e.g. Whitwell Common, Booton Common and Reepham Moor) are wet and marshy and provided grazing for cattle.

A further complication to understanding the origins of modern Reepham arises from the complexities of the Norman manorial system. Domesday Book shows that each of the four vills was already subdivided by 1086. For example, in Hackford William de Warenne held the main manor which Wither held in 1066 and Berner, the Crossbowman, held a small manor of about 120 acres which had formerly belonged to a freeman. Reepham only gains a mention in Domesday Book under the lands of Ralph Bainard: 'men in Reepham appertain to this (i.e. Kerdiston

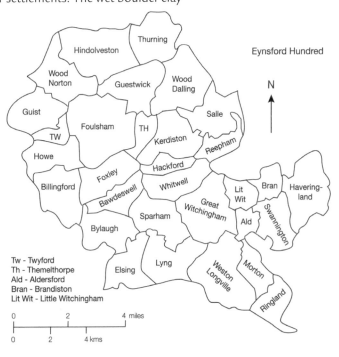

This map shows the parishes of Eynsford Hundred.

Eynsford Hundred

N ↑

Tw - Twyford
Th - Themelthorpe
Ald - Aldersford
Bran - Brandiston
Lit Wit - Little Witchingham

0   2   4 miles

0   2   4 kms

Manor) land and are assessed with this land'. It was the smallest of the four vills. The post Domesday manorial holdings of the four vills were:

> Kerdiston/Reepham
> Kerdiston/Calthorpes
> Hackford
> Hackford Ests and Thorpes
> Whitwell Gambons
> Whitwell Symonds
> Reepham Burgolions

The boundaries of these manors overlap the vill or parish boundaries. The relative simplicity of the great manors of East Dereham and North Walsham did not exist here. Indeed, Reepham seems to have as complicated a political geography as Harleston.

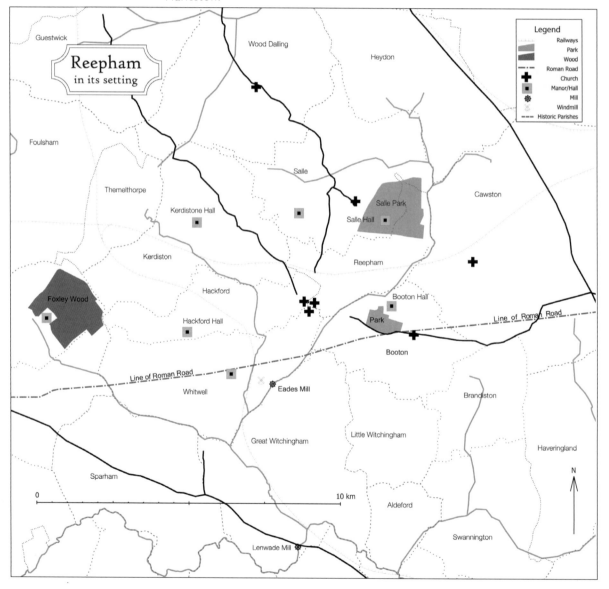

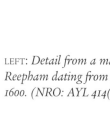

BELOW: *View east across the market place to the two churches.*

A few historical pegs exist on which some idea of the evolution of the area can be hung. The map shows that various manor sites and at least two village sites were focal points of settlements since gone. Faden, in 1797, marks both Kerdiston and Whitwell as demolished, implying that more settlement once existed. Alan Davison does not list them as deserted villages because various settlements have remained in both cases.[136] A market was established in Hackford in 1279, together with a fair; we can assume that the market place was in its present site because of the layout of the town around it.

ABOVE: *Sir William de Kerdiston's memorial in Reepham church.*

The cluster of three churches is a second clue to the concentration of settlement. Hackford had a church by 1086 and Kerdiston had a half church! No church was mentioned for Whitwell or Reepham but this does not necessarily mean that churches were not there. The architectural evidence of the churches of Hackford/Whitwell and Reepham/Kerdiston is negative as far as Saxon or Norman evidence is concerned. Pevsner and Wilson suggest that the south arcade of Reepham church dates to *c.* 1280. The great feature of Reepham church is the memorial to Sir William de Kerdiston, 1361. This is really the only link that the churches give us to major families of the area. The name de Kerdiston implies origins in Kerdiston and the choice of burial place in Reepham/Kerdiston church emphasises the connection. However, by 1199 the Kerdistons gained the manor and castle of Claxton and Kerdiston became one of their outlying manors. Map evidence suggests that the moated manor site at Kerdiston was later used as a rectory but whether this was the rectory for the chapel or for Reepham with Kerdiston church is not clear. In 1256 Whitwell church was given to Pentney Priory and thereafter its priests were vicars. A list of Whitwell vicars from 1321 and of Hackford rectors from 1317 suggests a coalescing of the settlements near to the church from the early 14th century.

BELOW: *The tower of Whitwell church.*

A second element in the evolution of the settlements is the establishment of mills. In 1086 Whitwell had three mills, Hackford one and Kerdiston an enigmatic quarter of a mill. The two small streams were useful and the mills at this date would be for grinding corn or possibly the fulling of cloth. Out of this complicated pattern of manors and parishes, served by their respective churches, the settlement which we now know as Reepham evolved.

The town

The town is focussed around the market place which lies to the west of the churchyard which once contained three churches. There is limited external evidence of timber framing in the buildings around it, which are largely built of red brick from 1700 onwards. As is so often the case, roads entering the market place approach it at various angles; that from Norwich twists round the churchyard and that from Cawston clips its west end. An attractive terrace edges the rest of the north side of the Market Place and the Bircham Institute frames the south-eastern edge. In 1542 Reepham, like nearly every other market town, suffered a fire, the chief effect of which was the destruction of Hackford church.

As has been noted in some of the other towns, no manor house, castle or monastic house exercised any influence over the development of the town. Outside it, Whitwell Hall was built around a 17th century core; Hackford Hall was built for Archdeacon Collyer in the 18th century; Kerdiston Hall replaced an earlier derelict moated site. The parish of Reepham had no major building in it but an attractive row of farmhouses lies along the north edge of Reepham Moor on which their cattle could graze.

Some idea of the earlier layout and nature of Hackford market comes from a late 17th century court book.[137] The entries show what pieces of land were recorded as valuable parts of the manor. For example, in 1738 Samuel Knowles, on a fine of 20s, took over from his father, Daniel Knowles, who was admitted in 1697.

> *To one parcel of ground containing in length 30ft and in breadth 15ft with a certain house thereon built and to one shop to the said house belonging and containing in length 12ft and in breadth 10ft and to another house to the said house belonging 7ft by 9ft and to a certain parcel of ground to the said house belonging and adjoining containing in length 18ft and in breadth 12ft lying, being in the market of Hackford aforesaid.*

ABOVE LEFT: *The Bircham Institute.*

ABOVE RIGHT: *A Georgian farmhouse on the edge of Reepham Moor, photographed in 1971.*

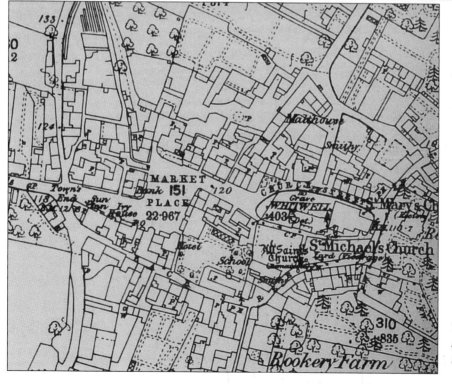

The centre of Reepham, as shown in the Ordnance Survey plan of 1886.

The tiny shops and stalls lay in front of messuages and tenements themselves only 30 feet deep and 6 feet wide. They may well have all been stalls originally before newer small shops replaced them as in North Walsham. Perhaps this was the infilling between Back Lane and the original market.

David Minns, a butcher who was admitted in 1750 to the manorial holding of a small market shop, died in 1762 and his inventory survives.[138] His property contained a saloon, a kitchen, a scullery, a brewhouse, pantry, cellar, landing, parlour chamber, chamber over the pantry and kitchen chamber. The landing implies that there was a staircase and the house had three upstairs rooms (chambers). In these premises was a shop with scales, a beam, brass and lead weights, three cleavers and a chopping block etc.

Outside the house was a barn, a pigsty with a sow and three pigs, a slaughter house, a hog sty and pound for beasts. The 59 sheep and the turnips they were feeding on were by far the biggest item, worth £42. The total value of his inventory was £115 2s 6d, that of a modest yeoman. David's house was certainly not one of the small properties mentioned in the court book but it gives some idea of the level at which a mid-century butcher lived.

Tanning and brewing

Tanning was an important rural industry in certain areas in the 18th and 19th centuries.[139] There were tanners in the Reepham area before the development of the three bigger tanneries. Edward Starke of Whitwell, tanner, left a will in 1633.[140] Edward left a little money to Whitwell church and its poor and £8 a year to his wife. He referred to his lands in Whitwell and Hackford and he left £50 and £5 to his daughter. Finally he left 'all my goods and chattels, my fats [vats] and leather and other things belonging to my trade to Edward Starke [his son] to pay my debts', that is, out of his income from the tannery Edward was to clear any debts.

Tanning only became 'industrialised' in rural areas in the late 18th century. Before that, outside bigger centres such as Norwich, individual farms would have had one or two tan pits for small scale leather production. There was great demand for leather for shoemaking, horse harness, clothing and up-market furnishings such as wall coverings. After tanning, skins went on to curriers who prepared the various leathers and then on to cordwainers (shoemakers), harness makers and so on. The production of leather needed a good supply of cattle and horse skins and of sheepskins from the fellmongers. It needed a good water supply

ABOVE: *Only the Cardinal's Hat in Back Street has a jetty and 16th century timber framing exposed.*

*Was Back Street (*BELOW LEFT*) the original southern boundary of the market, and were the King's Arms (*BELOW RIGHT*) and its western neighbours later infill? If so, the process must have begun in the 17th century to judge by the back range of the King's Arms.*

for several stages of processing which had to be kept clear of streams to avoid pollution. Finally, it needed large quantities of oak bark which was used in the steeping process to strengthen the water which had already had animal dung and urine added to it.

The wet plateau of the Kerdiston, Hackford and Salle area carried much woodland and land for cattle grazing. In the four parishes tanneries developed in Hackford Vale (the Bircham family *c.* 1700-1800), Whitwell Hall (the Leamon family *c.* 1800-80) and Whitwell Common (the Leeds family *c.* 1800-78). An inventory for Samuel Bircham gives some idea of his scale of business in 1779.[141] He was a wealthy man with a farm carrying 83 sheep and four cows, he had barley in the barn and some unsold turnips but his main wealth lay in his tannery which included the following list of his stock:

199 sole hides — hides at 45s each	*£ 447 15s 0d*
177 hides at 26s each	*230 2s 0d*
15 horse hides at 11s	*8 5s 0d*
84 skins (i.e. sheep skins) at 7s	*29 8s 0d*
Total	*£ 750 10s 0d*
Deduct for tanning duty and wages	*187 0s 0d*
Net value for the above stock	*528 10s 0d*
Bark in different barns — 48 loads at £6	*288 0s 0d*
Tanning utensils — hair, dry turf, lime etc.	*37 17s 0d*
Approximate value of tanning stock	*855 7s 0d*
Total inventory	*£1,462 14s 0d*

It is not clear exactly when the Birchams decided that brewing was a better bet than tanning but the next stage in their progression was to become brewers.

However, two other tanneries were established at Whitwell. The first in the grounds of the Hall by Robert Leamon. The evolution of this tannery and its layout has been well documented.[142] The second tannery was established by the Leeds family on the edge of Whitwell Common. The end of the Leamon tannery came as the result of a great fire which was recorded vividly in the *Norfolk Chronicle* of Saturday, 12th May 1877.

A fire of an alarming and destructive character occurred on the premises of Robert Leamon Esq. at Whitwell on Monday afternoon. It is supposed that a spark from the boiler flue fell upon one of the bark stacks situated to the south of the tannery, the flames soon communicating to the other stacks, only a few yards apart, and in a short time four stacks containing about 1200 tons of bark, were enveloped in flames. The

TOP: *Dial House (now called the Old Brewery) is the dominant building on the north side of the market place; it was originally the home of the Bircham family. The Chimes (*ABOVE*) makes a nice west end to the market area.*

BELOW LEFT: *Whitwell Hall.*

BELOW: *Kerdiston Hall.*

Whitwell Hall and the tannery: plan based on the tithe map of 1840 (NRO 862).

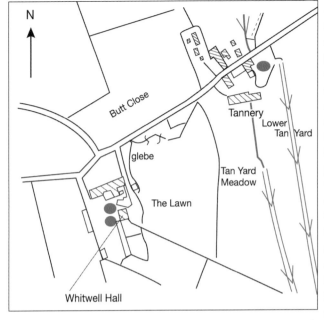

loss is estimated to about £6000 which we understood was only partly covered by insurance. There were a great number of men in Mr Leamon's employ, and immediately the alarm was given, every exertion was made to arrest the progress of the fire . . . One of the Reepham fire engines was quickly on the spot and their efforts were concentrated on the stack nearest the buildings, which fortunately were prevented from taking fire, but had the wind been blowing in a contrary direction the utmost efforts could not have saved the tannery buildings. The Aylsham engine soon followed . . . other engines arrived soon after. Several times during the evening the sparks from the burning stacks communicated with the stockyard and stables about five hundred yards in a direct line with the wind . . . a large number of people soon assembled and every assistance was rendered by willing hands amongst the foremost of whom was Mr Chambers, superintendent, Inspector Sowter and a large body of police, several of whom with the firemen and a number of Mr Leamon's men were left in charge of the burning stacks during the night.

Despite appeals for fresh supplies of bark the tannery only survived for another three years by which time the opening up of the mid west in the USA and the South American pampas lands being built by British-built railways and the invention of steamships led to the importing of animal hides from both areas and small tanneries could not compete.

The Bircham brewery dominated the north side of Reepham market place and the Brewery House remains as the dominant building there. The deeds of Reepham brewery were deposited in the Norfolk Record Office by Watney Mann in the 1980s.[143] The earliest reference in these deeds is to 1807 when William Bircham the younger married Charlotte Bartell of Holt and in agreeing to pay £2,000 to William Bartell reference was made

The pond which supplied water for the tanning mill: a photograph taken in 1995.

to the mansion, stables, brewery and a malting office.[144] In 1853 William Bircham the younger left Charlotte £1,000 per annum, a property in Yarmouth and The Ollands, their new built house in Reepham, for life. The brewery went to his nephew William Bircham. In 1878 the mansion and brewery was sold to H. S. Patteson and H. Bullard, Norwich brewers, by William and Marianne Bircham. So in 1877 the Leamon tannery fire took place, in 1878 the brewery was sold and in 1879 the Leeds tannery closed. The industrial base of Reepham's economy was shattered.

Reepham is now a very pleasant market town; new estates have not yet been added to it as severely as they have in other Norfolk towns. It is a commuting community with a much improved high school with a new sixth form. It is probably the town in this study that was least changed by the 20th century.

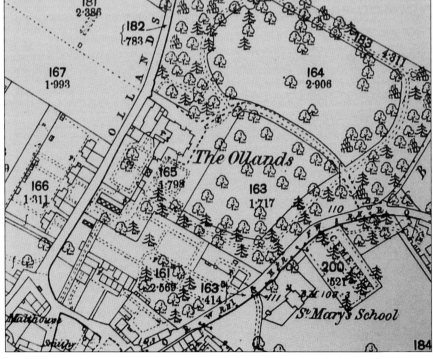

The Ollands, built for the Bircham family with the profits from their brewing operation. The map extract is from the Ordnance Survey's 1886 mapping and shows the house standing in over 13 acres of park and gardens, with a carriage drive approaching the house from the Norwich Road.

Swaffham chronology

5000–1500 BC	Neolithic farming
1500–500 BC	Bronze Age activity
500 BC – AD 50	Iron Age
AD 50–400	Roman occupation, Peddars Way
600	Saxon settlement at Swaffham, Saxon place name
870–1010	Danish invasions: Danes burn Thetford and Norwich
1066	Norman Conquest, William gives Swaffham to Earl Ralph
1086	William gives Swaffham to Alan of Richmond, Swaffham in the Honour of Richmond
1214	Market charter
1253	Grant of two fairs
1450	Swaffham and Norwich complain of Heydon and Tuddenham's flocks on the commons
1475	Camping Land given by Rev. John Botwright
1487	Simon Blake gave the Town Estate to Swaffham
1600–1700	Churchwardens' accounts give picture of life in Swaffham
1700–1800	Swaffham the social centre of west Norfolk
1725	Foundation of Hamond's School
1770	Norwich to Swaffham turnpike
1775	Fire around the White Hart
1783	Market cross built by the Earl of Orford
1788	A plague of locusts – 313 bushels of locusts gathered
1797	Faden's map of Swaffham
1801	Population 2,220
1817	Assembly Rooms built
1838	National School
1840	Gas works established
1841	Population 3,358
1847	Railway to London opened (closed 1964)
1850	Corn Hall built
1867	Waterworks established
1868	Swaffham enclosure award: 2,370 acres of heath enclosed
1888	Victoria Cottage Hospital opened
1891	Population 3,636
1895	Hamond's School moves to Market Place
1898	Swaffham Urban District Council formed
1901	Population 3,371
1951	Population 2,863
1974	Breckland District Council established
2001	Population 6,935

Swaffham

Unlike several of the other towns in this study, Swaffham can boast no castle, no monastery and not even a fine manor house. Why is it here? W. C. Southwell[145] echoed by W. G. Clarke[146] comments on the lack of surface water and points out that in the drought of 1864, despite wells 160 feet deep, Swaffham had to bring in water from Castle Acre and Narborough. When the Swaffham Water Board was established in 1869 its wells were sunk into the chalk to a depth of 180 feet. Southwell refers to Swaffham as the 'Montpelier of England' and noted that it was elevated 210 feet above sea level and the air pure and healthy and that 66 people who died between 1790 and 1890 had lived to between 90 and 102 years old. Perhaps the deep chalk wells may have ensured pure water. The Domesday Book entry mentions one and a half mills and a fishery and it is difficult to visualise where these were on this dry chalk plateau.

However, the archaeological evidence[147] shows that Swaffham had a large Anglo-Saxon cemetery under the present Paddocks estate off Haspalls Road. Nineteen burials were discovered in what is known to be only a part of a large burial ground. Where the related Saxon settlement was is less certain.

Aerial view of Swaffham church and market place.

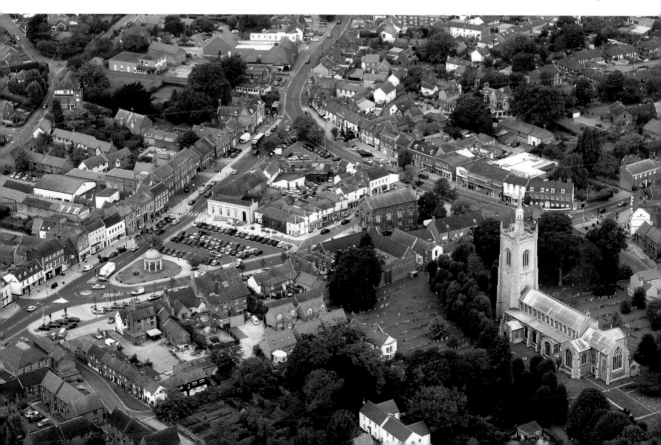

So there is no river, no crossing point, no striking valley site (as for example at Castle Acre three miles to the north). The Peddars Way lies two miles to the east of Swaffham but Castle Acre straddles it. Castle Acre would seem to have been much the better sited of the two settlements. Once Bishops Lynn was founded in 1101 communications between Swaffham and the Bishop's seat in Norwich and between merchants of the two towns must have become important.

Castle Acre was a de Warenne holding and it was the capital for the 145 manors that the de Warennes held in north-west Norfolk. Its castle was the centre of much activity and its Cluniac priory added to its importance. Swaffham, however, lay within the honour of Richmond and this royal control, together with the founding of a market by 1214 and two fairs in 1253 confirmed the importance of post-Conquest Swaffham which lay a day's travel from Dereham but a very good day's travel from Lynn.

Swaffham's privileges under the honour of Richmond were sufficient for a busy market town with its important parish church to develop. How many people lived in Swaffham in 1086? According to Domesday Book it had eight villagers and 25 smallholders, Dereham had 16 and 25, respectively and Sporle, near Swaffham, had 20 villagers, having had 32 in 1066. So Swaffham was not a particularly big settlement. It was spacious, being one league by one league (1.5 by 1.5 miles). Much of the land was heathland and, as might be expected on the chalk plateau, there was little woodland but the demesne farm had 200 sheep and the tenants would have had their own flocks as well.

Faden's plan of Swaffham, included in his map of Norfolk produced in 1797, shows the large market place which lay at a T junction with the Lynn to Norwich road. This cut its north end and the main axis of the market place followed the line of the London road which continued northwards as the road to Castle Acre. This is an example of a classic crossroads market place.

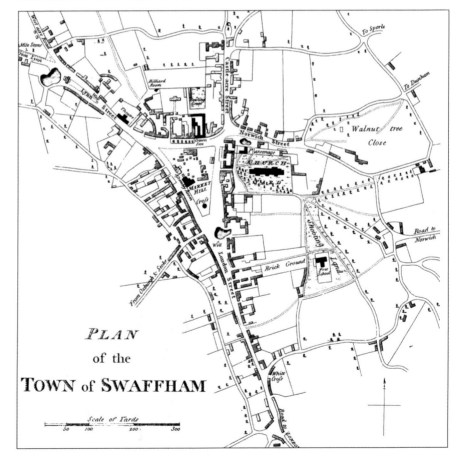

Swaffham occupations as revealed by wills and inventories			
	1500–1599	1600–1649	1650–1699
Bricklayer/maker	X		
Carpenter	X	X	
Glazier		X	
Painter		X	
Tailor			X
Draper	X		X
Mercer	X		
Merchant	X		
Baker	X	X	X
Brewer			X
Butcher		X	X
Fishmonger	X		
Innholder	X		
Innkeeper			X
Cordwainer	X		X
Glover	X	X	
Tanner		X	
Blacksmith	X	X	
Ironmonger	X		
Pewterer		X	
Gardener			X
Roper			X
Apothecary	X		
Barber	X		
Doctor/surgeon	X		
Sailor/boatman	X		
Weaver	X		X
Worsted trades			X

Even by the collection of the 1379 poll tax, a tax of 4d on every person over 16, Swaffham had only 84 taxpayers compared with Dereham's 381, North Walsham's 325 and Downham Market's 108. No comparable listing is given for Castle Acre.[148] We learn that Swaffham's two wealthiest taxpayers in 1379 paid only two shillings each, placing them in the artificers' category. They were Thomas Wombe and Johannes Bachiller. No other occupations are recorded in the Swaffham list.

As documentary sources improve, fresh gleams of light appear about the population of Norfolk's market towns. John Pound, in a detailed piece of statistical work, looked at wills and inventories for Norfolk from 1500 to 1699.[149] An extract from Pound's Table 1.2 shows the occupations for which Swaffham wills and inventories exist. Only bakers and cordwainers are noted in all three columns. Only in the 16th century are an apothecary, barber and doctor/surgeon recorded. Given all that has been said about the dryness of the area, a sailor/boatman is a little surprising!

Even as late as 1797 there was very little depth to development. The long axes of

Swaffham church.

properties lined the market rather than running end on to it. This suggests only a modest pressure on space. As with Dereham, the church lies back from the market place; was this perhaps once larger?

To the west of the town a back lane provided a service lane to the plots running back from the market. The market place has gradually been infilled in a triangular area at its north end.

Swaffham church

'The church at Swaffham is both one of the grandest and best documented building projects of 15th century Norfolk.'[150] Heslop's article gives the story of its stylistic sequence very clearly. Exceptionally a record of much of the rebuilding of this church survives in the famous *Black Book of Swaffham*.[151] In this it is pointed out that repairs to damage, that is of the old church, were in progress in 1456 when a bell tower, not the present one, was being repaired. By the early 1500s, however, the church was much as it exists now and the names of its major benefactors were John Chapman and his wife Catherine who gave £120, Simon Blake and his wife Jane, John Bladsmith, John Walsingham, Robert Payn, Walter Taylor and his wife Isobel and 50 lesser benefactors. As Heslop comments, 'this was clearly a community enterprise involving at least a tenth of the adult population'.

The pressure on population to contribute must have been considerable; 'strikingly absent from the lists of benefactors are any great lords'.[152] Heslop concludes that Swaffham was in no sense a backwater. Control over the town was exercised and contested by a number of wealthy aristocrats, courtiers and government officials some of whom, such as John Botwright, the vicar, were involved in building projects elsewhere and one of whom, Edmund Blake, had been clerk of the king's works. Yet it was the next tier of society in Swaffham that paid for the rebuilding of its church.

A church built on the scale of Swaffham and dependent on a wide range of benefactors was obviously an important centre for the parish and the community.

As in so many medieval churches a number of guilds existed; each guild served a particular craft or section of the community. Swaffham's guilds were: the Guild of the Ascension, St Nicholas, St Peter, St Helen, St John the Baptist, St Thomas a Becket the Martyr and of the Holy Trinity.

A little pamphlet on the guilds of Swaffham commented that 'of the guilds of Swaffham very little is known except their names, the particular minutes and other evidences being irretrievably lost'.[153] This sad comment means that what might have been a valuable further help in picturing Swaffham life before the Dissolution has gone. One writer comments that the Guild of the Ascension held lands, the Guild of St Nicholas owned valuable chalices and that the Guild of St John the Baptist had in 1485 seventy seven members, both men and women, who paid 3s 4½d, annual subscription. Guilds often had houses bequeathed to them and these, in some cases, became referred to as Guildhalls and they were appropriately enlarged for their social gatherings. No Swaffham guildhall has been discovered but each guild had its own altar in the church and that of the Holy Trinity had its own chapel in the new church.

Much of the social fabric of Swaffham, like that of so many other market towns of the 15th century, was structured around the church. In Swaffham's case the new church, like that of St Peter Mancroft in Norwich, was a communal effort. The churchwardens supervised the maintenance of the fabric as well as looking after the poor and sick until the Tudor overseers of the poor increasingly took on this role and raised a new poor rate additional to the churchwardens' annual rate. The surveyor of the highways also came under the authority of the vestry as did the parish constables.

Angels look down from the double hammerbeam roof of Swaffham church, as they have done for more than 500 years.

Churchwardens' accounts

Churchwardens' accounts survive sporadically and Swaffham is fortunate that long runs have been kept and a very helpful transcription of those for 1623–53 has been made.[154] Even in one year's account a surprising number of details of early

17th century Swaffham are revealed. George Gentleman was paid two shillings for pulling the stocks out of the pond! Flags were being cut and paid for by the parish to provide Widow Elwer with fuel, as they were also to warm the children taught by Widow Skelton, rye straw was used for thatching the well house by the common pool and to thatch Amy Gray's house, presumably an almshouse. Two more wells were mentioned; one was repaired in the marketstead and another thatched on Pickenham road. The importance of these wells emphasises the lack of surface water.

In November 3½ yards of russet cloth were paid for to make Otley's daughter a suit, 3 yards of cloth to make her a smock and she was provided with a pair of shoes. Eight pence were paid to Matthew Bishop when sick and sixpence to 'those that did watch with him'. The workmen repairing Swaffham's roads were provided with a barrel of beer and there are several references to helping the sick and one or two to helping poor soldiers.

Finally there are many references to the town's flock of 500 sheep; it cost the town 12s to have them clipped and 2s 8d to feed the clippers. Boys helped to shear them, shepherd them and wash them in the 'lock'.

The town farm

Swaffham was also fortunate to have a town farm which was a further responsibility of the churchwardens and later on of 12 senior members of the town as well. A series of carefully drawn up leases between the churchwardens and tenant farmers throw some light on how a breckland (heath) farm was worked.[155] The earliest lease was for 1722 when the farm was let to Mr Large for five years at an annual rental of £40. The farm's closes lay two miles west of Swaffham and were of several acres each, there was a foldcourse (sheep run) for the town flock and pieces (closes) in the open fields of Swaffham and it included the Camping Land. Strangely the size of the flock is not specified but it had a value of £110 and is presumably that of the 500 sheep mentioned earlier. By a lease of 1837 to a Mr Howarth it was said the flock must be not less than six score (120) and not more than 12 score (240) sheep inclusive of the shepherd's sheep. By this date the lease was very specific, stipulating that a sheep fold of four dozen common hurdles might stay only one night on one place. Even in 1722 the churchwardens were careful to point out that the sheep could only be folded on town farm land; this was to maintain the fertility of the town farm land.

The breck nature of the land was emphasised by the fact that the farmer was to pay a further £5 in rent if he brought land into cultivation that had not been worked for ten years in which time it should have recovered. In his last year Mr Large had to sow ten acres with turnips and prepare 18 acres of land so that the churchwardens or their tenants could use them and on which the sheep had to be tathed (kept to manure the land). By 1837 the rent was £170 per annum and the tenant had to sow 24 acres with seed grass every year and then no more than one crop of corn could be grown without summer tilling and then sowing the turnips followed by grass. In his last year the farmer had to sow 24 acres with turnips. The maintenance of soil fertility was a prime aim.

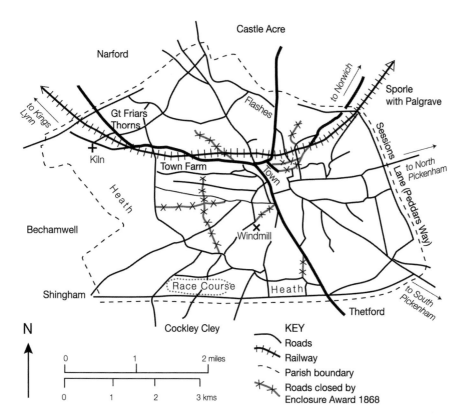

Swaffham's landscape was redesigned over considerable areas and many roads were closed once the need to serve commons or systems of arable strips were removed. This map shows the parish as it was in 1824, with the later railway line added.

The commons

Swaffham's commons, some 3,000 acres of them, survived until the Enclosure Act of 1878 but they were not without problems before this. It is by accident that gleams of light are thrown on the history of parishes and in 1450 one such example appears. This is in Volume II of the famous Paston letters.[156] Various power struggles were taking place in Norfolk during the chaotic period of the Wars of the Roses in the reign of Henry VI. One such struggle was between Sir Thomas Tuddenham of Oxburgh, John Heydon of Baconsthorpe and the City of Norwich. The people of Swaffham were suffering from Sir Thomas who, as the 'farmer' of the manor of Swaffham and bailiff, was misbehaving. On 20th December 1450 a letter from no less than Sir John Fastolf to Sir Thomas Howys (the Paston servant) referred to a letter he had received from Maister John Botewrighte, the eminent rector of Swaffham, complaining that

> grete extorcion have been done by the offices of the Duchie in takyng away 90 acres pasture at Swaffham which is of the King's demesnes and of hys enheritaunce as of the Duchee of Lancaster, for whych pastures yff it can not . . . it will be . . . of final destruction of the tenauntes there'. The inhabitants of Swaffham were so concerned that they drafted a petition to parliament, which was not in fact presented but in its last lines pleaded that the King and Lords 'commit the said Sir Thomas Tuddenham to preson, there to abide till in to the tyme that he to the said inditements hath answered, and to the billes and compleynts of the said inhabitants in forume of law.

Although it was not specifically stated it is probable that Tuddenham and

Contrasting styles and materials in Swaffham architecture:

TOP TO BOTTOM: *Two styles of Georgian brick façades; the east side of the market place; the north end of the market place at the junction of the Norwich and Castle Acre roads; orange brick and slate contrasting with flint and pantiles.*

BELOW: *Flint, edged with brick moulding.*

Heydon had been putting their own flocks of sheep on great stretches of Swaffham's commons because wool was one of the main sources of wealth in Norfolk. As Sir Thomas Tuddenham was acting lord of the manor he would be in a good position to overstock the commons with his sheep thereby reducing the nibble for the commoners' sheep. It was complained that he had been doing this for 16 years.

One can understand the concern of Swaffham's manorial tenants when we look at the links with sheep management as part of their economy. Simon Blake, in his will of 1489, left his wife and Richard Bocking 60 adult sheep and 60 lambs.[157] In 1496 Richard Styward left a long will with many acres of land to his son Thomas in specific closes and in the fields of Swaffham and 'the liberty of my fold' (that is, his right to run a flock of sheep).[158]

The significance of sheep in the Swaffham economy may have been the reason for the very late parliamentary enclosure of the parish in 1863. Over much of it grazing rights for the sheep after harvest led to a half-year system operating. This allowed common grazing over fields that were rented for cropping only. This was finally sorted out by a massive enclosure act in 1863. The commissioner had to allocate land in lieu of half-year rights in a very complex award.

Amongst the major allotments made by the commissioner a public pond was awarded underlining the need for surface water and the churchwardens and overseers received 55 acres in three pieces. Smallholders in Swaffham with cottages and gardens generally received about ten times their cottage area in allotments in lieu of their loss of grazing, fuel and gravel rights. Anthony Hamond, lord of Swaffham manor, received 153 acres of the heath and eight acres of Lynn Scoot and the Splashes.

Swaffham in the 18th century

A thriving market town such as Swaffham, like others discussed in this study, gradually developed an increasingly complex social fabric as local benefactors appeared and as central government began to expect hundreds and parishes to take on certain social responsibilities. The first of the benefactors founded a grammar school for the town.

In 1725 Nicholas Hamond, obviously a wealthy man, left £300 a year for five years out of his Swaffham estate for charitable uses. Trustees, mainly local clergy, were to use the first £500:

> In erecting a building convenient for the dwelling of a master and his family and for a schoolroom for instructing and teaching 20 youths to read the English tongue and a room or rooms for the convenient employing 20 poor persons to work in the manufacture of this county to be provided for them which said building I desire may be erected at the south end of the close commonly called the Camping Land . . . or some other convenient place.[159]

A second £500 was then to be spent buying land to support the school and the final £500 to cover running costs to clothe the 40 children in the school and workhouse. Presumably Nicholas meant spinning and/or weaving in referring to the manufacture of this county. An inventory taken in 1768 of the contents of the workhouse listed 16 spinning wheels and five reels amongst its contents. Given the

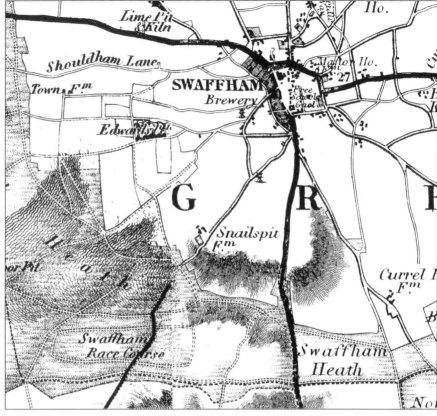

Bryant's map of 1826 shows Swaffham race course on the heath to the south-west of the town.

The Assembly Rooms in Swaffham were built in the late 18th century for social functions, and restored in the early 21st century for very similar purposes.

growth of factory spinning in Lancashire and Yorkshire by this time it was almost too late to try and bring up a new generation with these skills.[160]

Swaffham had become an important social centre for the west of Norfolk by the 18th century. A race course was established for the entertainment of the local gentry and in 1755 on Tuesday 23rd September Swaffham races were held for a plate of £50. The stewards were Sir A. Wodehouse Bart. and Francis Lombe Esq. It was advertised:

> As for 14 hands to carry 8 stone 7 lbs, higher or lower weight in proportion; the best of three 4 mile heats. Wednesday, the 24th a plate of £50 for any horse, mare or gelding the property of a subscriber to these plates or an inhabitant of the counties of Norfolk and Suffolk that has actually been used as a regular hunter last season but has not been in sweats from the 1st November to Lady Day last and has never won any plate but a hunter's. Six year olds to carry 11 stone . . . At this meeting will be a sweepstake to be rode by gentlemen and a match between Lord Orford and Jennison Shaftoe Esq.[161]

The town suffered a major fire in 1775, which explains why so much of the architecture dates from the late 18th century.

How Swaffham was governed

Swaffham from 1086 lay within the honour of Richmond. The manor was held directly from the Crown and both court leets and courts baron were held by its lord. A bailiff and 12 jurors sat at the leet courts. The main manor had a subsidiary manor of Whitsands and Haspalls divided off from it by 1239. This was given to Swaffham by Simon Blake in 1487.[162]

Very importantly for Swaffham it gained its market charter in 1214 which was confirmed after opposition, rather surprisingly, from Great Dunham in 1253. In 1575 a market cross and house were built and this was rebuilt in 1783. By 1620 the market had 133 stalls and 14 shops. The service nature of Swaffham was increased by grants in 1253 for two fairs, one on 25th January (St Paul) and the other on 29th June (St Peter).

Swaffham's market cross was erected by Horatio, 2nd Earl of Orford, in 1781–83.

As well as being an important royal manor Swaffham was a centre for county administration. The constable of the hundred of South Greenhoe was responsible to the sheriff of Norfolk and so to the Crown for the collection of national taxes such as subsidies and hearth taxes. So from the reign of Edward VI when the late medieval system of religious charities collapsed Swaffham was gradually to acquire structures for looking after problems of unemployment and hunger which resulted in the need to look after poor children, poor families and the sick. The organisation of county and district courts dealt increasingly firmly with those found guilty of crime and a structure of bridewells and a county prison in Norwich with national courts for extreme cases dealt with problems of riots as well as more domestic crises. These structures replaced those of the manor courts and the church courts held by the bishop and archdeacons.

Unlike the other market towns, with the exception of Downham Market, quarter sessions were held from time to time in Swaffham Cross and in 1659 the Cross and Sessions House were in disrepair. William Burleigh, Clerk of the Peace for Norfolk, instructed the hundreds to contribute a total sum of £30 for their repair. On 11th October 1659 he issued a receipt for £6 19 9*d*, being the money received from the hundreds of North Greenhoe, Smythdon, Launditch, West Flegg, Freebridge, Marshland, Happing and part of Grimshoe.[163] More was raised from two other groups of hundreds on 20th July and 10th January. The hundreds continued to have this role until 1834 when the new Poor Law system replaced the hundredal system which had survived for a thousand years.

The creation of a nationwide system of Poor Law Unions following the Poor Law Amendment Act of 1834 altered the local government patterns, especially in rural areas. The Swaffham Union workhouse was built outside the town on the Watton Road replacing an earlier town workhouse.

As one of the centres for the county's legal system Swaffham had a bridewell from 1599 which was replaced by a house of correction in 1787 and enlarged in 1821 and 1844. The Shirehall was built in 1839, Swaffham being the centre for elections for the west of the county. The health needs of the town were better looked after when the Victoria Cottage Hospital was built by public subscription in 1888 to mark Queen Victoria's jubilee and an isolation hospital in 1903.

The 1894 Local Government Act resulted in Swaffham having its own urban district council; this survived until 1974 when it was replaced by Breckland District Council. The administrative centre for Breckland District Council is, perhaps rather surprisingly, East Dereham.

Communications

Swaffham's links with other parts of the county were improved by the building of the Norwich to Swaffham turnpike in 1770. It is nearer to Lynn than to Norwich but this development must have done much to link Swaffham rather more firmly to Norwich. Amongst the first trustees of the Norwich to Swaffham turnpike were Jeremiah Ives Jnr, Mayor; Dr John Beevor, Nockold Thompson, all of Norwich; Edward Pratt Esq. of Ryston, Mr William Donne of Swaffham; John Fenn Esq, Mr Roger Duquesne, Charles Weston and Charles Townshend, Esq of the Dereham area.

By the seventh meeting contributions of £100 each were received from two Dereham inn holders and Edward Pratt. By the eighth meeting on 26th March 1781 further investors were Edward Cace, Mr Duquesne and Charles Gould. Various small pieces of land were purchased for road straightening in Scarning and Little Fransham. The minutes give vast detail of purchases of axes, shovels and barrows and details were given of claims for damage to crops. The minute book for 1785 to 1811 notes that at the 94th meeting on 5th December 1785 no trustees attended and it was adjourned to early January! At the 99th meeting Earlham tollgate was advertised to be let for £293 per annum but the current occupant finally got it for £329 per annum. By comparison the Mattishall gate was let for only £24, Scarning gate for £130 and Swaffham Gate for £57 in 1788.[164]

The second transport factor that changed the space relationships of market towns was the arrival of the railway and also the links that the railway emphasised. Though no turnpike was made to Lynn, Swaffham was linked to it by rail in 1844, then to Dereham by 1848 and to Thetford via Watton in 1875. No direct line was built from Norwich to Dereham and this must have been a disadvantage to both towns. Between 1844 and 1968 the Lynn line strengthened Swaffham's link with west Norfolk link which was so marked in the 18th century. The closure of the line in 1968 broke this link again but by this time the bus and car offset the break.

Swaffham market place, surrounded by its 18th century brick façades with its handsome church set behind it, is one of the least spoilt of all the towns being discussed. This is in part because the pressures on Swaffham have perhaps been less so far than on most of the other towns in this study.

The former railway station in Swaffham.

Notes

NRO = Norfolk Record Office

Attleborough

1   Blomefield, vol. 1, pp. 506–22.
2   Nikolaus Pevsner, *Essex*, p. 94.
3   J. C. Barringer, 'College House, Attleborough' *Bulletin of the Norfolk Research Committee* vol. 11 (1973), pp. 4–5.
4   J. T. Barrett, *Memorials of the Parochial Church . . . of Attleborough* (1848).
5   *Report of the Commissioners Appointed . . . to Enquire Concerning Charities.* 29th Report, pp. 826–9.
6   NRO: Wayland Union books, Vol. 1.
7   J. Ogilby, *Britannia* (London 1675; repr. Duckham, 1939), vol. 1, plate 46.
8   NRO: T3/7 Act 20 George II (1741).
9   NRO: T3/58 1860.
10   NRO: SPE 37, 315X5.
11   Gaymer's records in NRO: BR47.
12   Attleborough Enclosure Act 1812.

Aylsham

13   S. Bates and A. Shelley, 'Excavations in Red Lion Street, Aylsham 2003' (Norfolk Archaeological Unit Report) pp. 1, 2.
14   Aylsham Local History Society, *Aylsham in the Seventeenth Century* (Poppyland, 1988).
15   'Aylsham Sexton's Manor Custumal 1542' NRO: NRS 12403.27.D1, p. 5.
16   Aylsham Sexton's Court Book 1623–1660, NRO: NRS 16632 37G, folios 459, 460.
17   J. Turville Petre, 'The Tofts of Aylsham Manors', *Norfolk Archaeology* 42 (1995), pp. 148–59.
18   S. Cotton and P. Cattermole, 'Medieval Parish Church Building in Norfolk', *Norfolk Archaeology* XXXVIII, Pt III, 1983, p. 237.
19   This section draws heavily on a valuable article by Anne Sutton, 'The Early Linen and Worsted Industry of Norfolk and the Evolution of the London Mercers' Company', *Norfolk Archaeology* XL, Pt III (1989), pp. 201–23.
20   E. Ekwall, *Studies in the Population of Medieval London* (Stockholm: Almquist & Wiksell, 1956).
21   Aylsham Local History Society, *Aylsham in the Seventeenth Century* (Poppyland, 1988).
22   Aylsham Churchwardens' accounts 1637–1848. NRO: PD 602/70.
23   J. Sapwell, *History of Aylsham* (Aylsham, 1960).
24   T. Mollard (ed.), *Millgate, Aylsham, Norfolk* (Aylsham, 1993), p. 13.
25   *Millgate,* p. 13.
26   *Millgate,* p. 33.
27   Will of William Parmeter of Aylsham, flour merchant, 1793. NRO: NCC 86 Stills.

Diss

28　NRO: PD100/263.

29　Articles of Enquiry relating to the Extent and Customs of the Manor of Diss. NRO: PD100/326.

30　A tilt was a canvas cover: D. Yaxley, *A Researcher's Glossary* (Larks Press, 2003), p. 217.

31　Customs of the parish of Diss. NRO: MS 17566.

32　Blomefield, vol. 1, p. 19.

33　NRO: MS 17589, 38D.

34　Accounts of the Guildhall 1780–1846. NRO: PD100/358.

35　7 Inventories 1696 to 1795. NRO: PD 100/140.

36　Diss Constable's account for 1836. NRO: PD 100/257.

37　N. Evans, *The East Anglian Linen Industry* (Gower/Passold, 1985), maps 3 and 4, remapped for the Diss area.

38　Arthur Young, *A General View of the Agriculture of the County of Norfolk* (London, 1804), pp. 326–7, David & Charles Reprints, 1969

39　William Marshall, *The Review and Abstract of the County Reports to the Board of Agriculture* Vol 3 Eastern Department (1818; reprinted New York: Kelley, 1968), p. 386.

40　Conveyance and papers of Dyson's purchase of Diss Brewery, 1801. NRO: MC 257/106/1–3.

41　Inventory and valuation of the brewing utensils. NRO: MC 257/106/1/3, 751X1.

42　Prospectus for the intended Diss and Bungay Junction Navigation Company. NRO: MEA 8/11, 661X3.

Downham Market

43　D. Dymond, 'Medieval and Later Markets' in *An Historical Atlas of Norfolk,* 3rd ed (Chichester: Phillimore, 2005), pp. 76–7.

44　A. Davison, 'A Moated Rectory at Wimbotsham, Norfolk' (East Anglian Archaeology Occasional Paper 12) (2003).

45　Timothy L. M. Hawes, *The Inhabitants of Norfolk in the Fourteenth Century: The Lay Subsidies of 1327 and 1332,* (Norfolk Historical Aids, 14, 17, 20, 23 & 26) (Norwich: the author, 2001).

46　Hawes, vol. 5.

47　Downham Subsidy List for 15 Henry VIII 1523/4. NRO: Bradfer Lawrence BL XIb book 3, 106–12.

48　Correspondence with reference to setting up Butter Market. NRO: Hare 643/5, 118X2.

49　Downham Field Book, 1629. NRO: MS 505.

50　NRO: NCC Inv 67 (B) 1697/8.

51　NRO: ANF/11/5 90, 1754/74.

52　Nikolaus Pevsner & Bill Wilson, *Norfolk 2: North-west and South* (Penguin, 1999), pp. 308–9.

53　41 George III c. 46, 21 May 1801.

54　Downham Market Union Records, First Minute Book 24 August 1836 to 19 July 1838. NRO: C/GP/5.

55　Downham Market School Board minutes, 1871 to 1879. NRO: C/Ed3/64.

East Dereham

56　*Liber Eliensis* (1169).

57　*Domesday Book Norfolk* 2 ed. Philippa Brown (Chichester: Phillimore, 1984), p. 214.

58　E. Miller, *The Abbey and Bishopric of Ely* (Cambridge University Press, 1951), p. 31.

59　N. Boston and E. Puddy, *Dereham: the Biography of a Country Town* (Dereham, 1952).

60　Register of the Bishop of Ely and survey of Dereham in Cottonian Mss. Claudius folios 221–33, in Blomefield, vol. 10, pp. 204–7.

61 D. W. Hollis, 'A mid-seventeenth century view of East Dereham manor', *Norfolk Archaeology* XXXVI, Pt 4 (1977), pp. 342–54.

62 Hollis, as above.

63 NRO: NCC Inventory 82/161, 1754.

64 A rand was 'a strip of leather in the heel of a shoe, turned over and seamed to strengthen it': J. G. Nall, *Nall's Glossary of East Anglia Dialect* (Dereham: Larks Press, 2006).

65 N. Boston & E. Puddy, *Dereham: the Biography of a Country Town* (Dereham, 1952), pp. 66–9.

66 J. Barney, *The Norfolk Railway* (Mintaka Books, 2007), maps A3 and A5.

67 Boston and Puddy, pp. 68–70.

68 Ben Norton, *The Story of East Dereham* (Chichester: Phillimore, 1994), p. 29.

69 Boston and Puddy, p. 200.

Fakenham

70 S. Cotton & P. Cattermole, 'Medieval Parish Church Building in Norfolk, *Norfolk Archaeology* XXXVIII Part 3 (1983), p. 246.

71 Francis Blomefield, *An Essay towards a Topographical History of the County of Norfolk* continued by Charles Parkin (London, 1805–10), vol. 8, p. 96. All references are to this edition.

72 *The Victoria History of the County of Norfolk* vol. 2 (1905), pp. 382–3.

73 Field Book of 1659 transcribed by P. G. Bales. NRO: PD 204/101. The transcriptions of many Fakenham documents by P. G. Bales have been a very valuable source for this chapter.

74 Notes on the fire of 1659. NRO: PD 204/105.

75 Fire at Fakenham. NRO: PD 204/103.

76 NRO: MS 1972013 ZiG. These are primarily of the Civil War period and that of the fire.

77 NRO: NRS 19720/13.

78 Files of notes and papers re the history of Fakenham containing several transcriptions by P. G. Bales. NRO: PD204/140.

79 Wells to Fakenham Turnpike minutes. NRO: DC 18/4/1.

Harleston

80 Nikolaus Pevsner & Bill Wilson, *Norfolk 2: North-west and South* (Penguin, 1999), pp. 383–86.

81 J. Fairclough and M. Hardy, *Thornham and the Waveney Valley* (Heritage Marketing, 2004), pp. 25, 29, 35.

82 Sheppard Frere & Roy Rainbird Clarke, 'The Romano-British village at Needham, Norfolk', *Norfolk Archaeology* XXVIII (1945), pp. 187–216; Clarke, 'Brettenham and Needham', *Norfolk Archaeology* XXVI (1937), 123–63 (map between pp. 162 and 163).

83 Blomefield, vol. V, pp. 376–7 and 380.

84 Particular of Sale of Manors (by Dukes of Norfolk). NRO: NRS 5721, 18C2.

85 Typescript notes on Mendham Priory, *c.* 1900. NRO: PD295/174.

86 A full architectural description of the church is in Pevsner & Wilson, vol. 2, p. 609.

87 S. Cotton and P. Cattermole, 'Norfolk Church Building', *Norfolk Archaeology* XXXVIII, Part 3 (1983), p. 261.

88 NRO: PD 295/55.

89 Faculty for new rectory at Redenhall. NRO: PD 295/35.

90 Gillingwater, *A Short Account of the Dissenting Congregation of Harleston*. NRO: PD 295/157.

91 NRO: MC 257/104/13.

92 *Oxford Dictionary of National Biography* (2004), vol.21.

93 NRO: MC 600/1 & 2, 780X9.

94 NRO: MC 600/8–12, 780X9.

Holt

95 L. B. Radford, *History of Holt* (Holt: Rounce & Wortley, 1908), p. 89

96 NRO: Executors of Cozens-Hardy 11.2.76, Holt Box.

97 This account of the town draws on Nikolaus Pevsner & Bill Wilson, *Norfolk 1: Norwich and North-East* (Buildings of England series) (Penguin, 1997), pp. 554–9, and S. Benson, *A Stroll through Georgian Holt* (Holt: Holt Society, 2006).

98 NRO: Executors of Cozens-Hardy 11.2.76, Holt Box.

99 T. W. Fanthorpe and A. Childs, *The Story of Holt Hall* (Halsgrove, 2007).

100 J. Smith & J. Pocock, *The Story of Holt* (Holt: Peacock Press, 1994).

101 Holt and Letheringsett Enclosure Award, extracts in longhand and a map redrawn from the original in 1934. NRO: C/Sca 2/165.

102 NRO Executors of Cozens-Hardy 11/2/76 Holt Box

103 T. W. Fanthorpe and A. Childs, *The Story of Holt Hall,* Halsgrove 2007, p. 21.

Loddon

104 Martin George, *The Land Use, Ecology and Conservation of Broadland* (Chichester: Packard, 1992), pp. 74, 358, 442.

105 East Anglian Archaeology report no. 49 (Dereham: Norfolk Archaeology Unit, 1990).

106 Alayne Fenner after Davison, *Evolution of Settlement,* pp. 41–57 in East Anglian Archaeology report no. 49.

107 NRO: MS 160441, 55x6.

108 There are many Domesday references to half mills, perhaps shared between two manors, but the Bury mill is recorded as one mill.

109 Pevsner & Wilson, *Norfolk 2,* p. 526.

110 Cotton & Cattermole, *Norfolk Archaeology* XXXVIII, Part III (1983), p. 254.

111 Mr Fuller's bill for glazing at Loddon Church. NRO: PD 595/84.

112 Feoffment of 1509 NRO MC 78/96/2 523x3

113 NRO: MC 78/96/04, 523x3.

114 NRO: MC 78/96/10, 523x3.

115 NRO: MC 78/96/16, 523x3.

116 NRO: MC 78/96/17, 523x3.

117 Churchwardens' vouchers 1857. NRO: PD 595/116.

118 Churchwardens' vouchers 1858/9. NRO: PD 595/117.

119 NRO: DCN/NDS/278.

120 NRO: PD 595/211.

North Walsham

121 Karl Inge Sandred, *The Place-names of Norfolk. Part 2. The Hundreds of East and West Flegg, Happing and Tunstead* (Nottingham: English Place-Name Society, 1996).

122 Sandred, p. 160.

123 James R. West, *St Benet at Holme 1020 to 1210: the Register of the Abbey of St Benet of Holme* (Norfolk Record Society vols 1 & 2), 1932.

124 St Benet's Register No. 276.

125 L. Redstone, 'The Cellarer's Account for Bromholm Priory, Norfolk, 1415–1416' in Norfolk Record Society vol. 17 (1944), pp. 47–92.

126 A. Dunn, *The Great Rising of 1381* (Tempus, 2002), pp. 129–33.

127 Bacon IV, 129.

128 North Walsham Court Book. Church Commissioners Bishops' Estates 1645–1659. NRO: C, 191.

129 NRO North Walsham Court Book A. 1611–1620.

130 *Norfolk Hearth Tax Assessment 1664* transcribed by M. S. Frankel and P. J. Seaman (Norfolk

& Norwich Genealogical Society, vol. 15) (1983), pp. 95–6.

131 C. Barringer (ed.), *North Walsham in the Eighteenth Century* (North Walsham WEA, 1983) and P. Warren (ed.), *North Walsham in the Nineteenth Century* (North Walsham WEA, 1993).
132 NRO Church Commissioners 164 364, 1767–1778, 291a
133 Warren, 74–76.

Reepham

134 Blomefield, vol. VIII, p. 244.
135 K. Cameron, *English Place Names* (Batsford, 1961), p. 191; M. Gelling, *Place Names in the Landscape* (Dent, 1984), p. 279.
136 Alan Davison, *Deserted Villages in Norfolk* (North Walsham: Poppyland, 1996).
137 Hackford market court book 1667. NRO: NRS 16786, 42F.
138 David Minns, butcher of Reepham. NRO: ANW 1754–67, No. 54.
139 C. Barringer, 'Tanners and tanning' in *An Historical Atlas of Norfolk,* 3rd ed. (Chichester: Phillimore, 2005), p. 160.
140 Will of Edward Starke, tanner 1633, NRo NCC 5 Tuck. MF/RO 201/1
141 Samuel Bircham of Hackford NRO 1779 NCC Inv
142 I. Mary Manning, 'Whitwell Hall Tannery: preliminary report', *Journal of the Norfolk Industrial Archaeology Society* vol. vol. 1 (1975), pp. 14–16 and 'Whitwell Hall Tannery' in vol. 3 (1983), pp. 102–6.
143 NRO: BR 155/1/3.
144 Deeds of Bircham brewery 1640–1927. NRO: BRA 1164/6, 760X3.

Swaffham

145 W. C. Southwell, *Our Town . . . Swaffham* (Swaffham: Willliam Gould, 1892).
146 W. G. Clarke, *Guide to the Town of Swaffham* (Swaffham, 1909).
147 P. Wade-Martins in *East Anglian Archaeology* 2 (1976), pp. 1–44.
148 R. C. Fenwick (ed.), *The Poll Taxes of 1377, 1379 and 1381, Part 2* (British Academy, 2001).
149 J. Pound, *Tudor and Stuart Norwich* (Chichester: Phillimore, 1988), Table 1.2.
150 T. A. Heslop, 'Swaffham Church' in *Medieval East Anglia* (ed. C. Harper-Bill) (Ipswich: Boydell, 2005), p. 256.
151 J. F. Williams, 'The Black Book of Swaffham', *Norfolk Archaeology* XXXIII (1965), pp. 243–53.
152 Heslop, p. 260.
153 WHK, *An Account of Swaffham Guilds.* NRO: PD 52/401.
154 Swaffham Churchwardens' Accounts 1623–53. Transcription. NRO: Col 13/173.
155 Swaffham Town Farm leases. NRO: PD 52/308/312.
156 *The Paston Letters 1422–1590*, Vol II, ed. James Gairdner (New York: Aims Press, 1965), pp. 197, 232.
157 Simon Blake, Will 1489. NRO: NCC 20–23 Typpes (MF31).
158 Richard Styward, Will 1496. NRO: NCC 11–12 Multon (MF32).
159 Copy of the will of Nicholas Hamond. NRO: DN MSC 3/24.
160 Inventory of goods in Swaffham Workhouse. Rix folder. NRO: PD52/404.
161 Newspaper cuttings 1753–55. NRO: MC 79/1, 522X5, fo. 8.
162 Blomefield, vol. VI, p. 202.
163 Papers re repair of Swaffham Market Cross and Sessions House. NRO: NCR Case 26, B/65.
164 Minute Book of the Swaffham Turnpike, October 1785 to February 1811. NRO: T2/3.

Index